Poems of
Robert Burns

Poems of
Robert Burns

*Selected and with an Introduction
by* IAN RANKIN

PENGUIN CLASSICS
an imprint of
PENGUIN BOOKS

Penguin [...] Published by the Penguin [...]
Penguin Books Ltd, 80 Strand, London WC2R 0RL, England

Penguin [...] USA [...] Hudson Street, New York, New York [...] USA
Penguin Group [...] Avenue East, Suite 700, Toronto, Ontario, Canada M4P 2Y3
[...] (a division of Pearson Penguin Canada Inc.)

Penguin Ireland, 25 St Stephen's Green, Dublin 2, Ireland
(a division of Penguin [...])

Penguin Group (Australia), 250 Camberwell Road, Camberwell, Victoria 3124, Australia
(a division of Pearson Australia Group Pty Ltd)

Penguin Books India Pvt Ltd, 11 Community Centre, Panchsheel Park, New Delhi – 110 017, India
Penguin Group (NZ), 67 Apollo Drive, Rosedale, North Shore 0632, New Zealand
(a division of Pearson New Zealand Ltd)
Penguin Books (South Africa) (Pty) Ltd, 24 Sturdee Avenue, Rosebank, Johannesburg 2196, South Africa

Penguin Books Ltd, Registered Offices; 80 Strand, London WC2R 0RL, England

www.penguin.com

This selection first published 2008

1

Selection and Introduction copyright © John Rebus Ltd, 2008

'The Fornicator', 'Ode to Spring' and 'Kirkcudbright Grace', from James Kingsley, ed.,
The Poems and Songs of Robert Burns, 3 vols, 1968, are reproduced by permission of
Oxford University Press

The moral right of the editor has been asserted

Set in 10/12.5pt Sabon by Palimpsest Book Production Limited, Grangemouth, Stirlingshire
Printed in Great Britain by Clays Ltd, St Ives plc

A CIP catalogue record for this book is available from the British Library

ISBN: 978-1-846-14116-4

www.greenpenguin.co.uk

Contents

Introduction

I grew up in the heart of the Fife coalfields. My hometown of Cardenden had barely existed (save as a church and some farms) until the discovery of local coal-seams. Early in the twentieth century families moved eastwards from Lanarkshire to Fife to claim their share of the new jobs. Houses were erected in a hurry – with no time even to think of names for the streets, so that they were called One Street, Two Street, Three Street, and so on. It was a community driven by hard work and common beliefs. The miners paid for local amenities to be constructed and even for an annual children's outing to the seaside. Little wonder that Robert Burns – the 'People's Poet', the voice of working-class Scotland – was revered.

In primary school, with the help of the local Burns Club, the children were persuaded to learn one of the bard's poems and one of his lyrics by heart. We were then taken to the church hall across the street and, in front of parents and dignitaries, led one at a time on to the stage to recite the one and sing the other. An elderly gentleman had been placed backstage and would take each of us by the hands, telling us not to be nervous and to fix our eyes on the large clock at the back of the hall, so as not to be distracted by the audience. Afterwards, certificates were awarded, with an additional gold-trimmed diploma for those who passed a written classroom test on Burns's life and work.

In a box somewhere, I probably still have all three.

The Scots remain proud of Robert Burns. He is known internationally, celebrated around the world at Burns Night ceilidhs and dinners. On New Year's Eve (called Hogmanay in Scotland) people link arms to sing the words of 'Auld Lang Syne' – whether or not they understand them. On a recent trip to Dunedin in New Zealand I was shown a large statue of the poet, dominating the main square. My guide was happy to point out that Burns had been positioned with his back to the church, but facing the pub. Yet much of Burns's output remains unread or under-appreciated. Some people consider him a populist, others a figure of romance. Many a Scot can probably recite the first few lines of 'To a Mouse' or 'To a Haggis', or sing the opening verse of 'A Red, Red Rose'. People know the story of 'Tam o' Shanter', but only the purists have the poem by heart. So just how relevant is Burns and why does he deserve his many memorials?

Robert Burns was a self-starter. He did not come from a privileged background, but was surrounded by the ballads, stories and songs of his native Ayrshire. As an adult, he failed (more than once) at his father's profession of farming, but seemed to find adversity a suitable muse. He was a profligate lover and his 'love' poems are artful constructions, often attempting to persuade the woman that Burns will always remember her, even though he is about to move on to fresher fare. In recent years, some of Burns's bawdier creations have been republished (see 'The Fornicator'), showing just how earthy he was. There's nothing fancy or high-handed about Burns, yet he is also capable of intellectual debate and political commentary. His poem 'Fareweel to a' Our Scottish Fame' is a sustained piece of controlled vitriol. The battlefield heroes of the past (Bruce and Wallace) have been betrayed by a 'coward few', bribed to bring Scotland under the yoke of England so that it becomes a mere 'province'. When I chose to preface my novel *Black and Blue* with a quote from Burns's poem, I did so because that book discussed the failed devolution vote of 1979 and the use of oil revenues as funding for the British government's campaign in the South Atlantic. (The Scottish National Party used often to campaign under the slogan-cum-rallying-cry 'It's Scotland's oil!')

Burns's lifetime coincided with a period of political turmoil. He looked at the French Revolution with great interest, and was a proponent of social equality. (Having given up farming for the life of a government exciseman, his positive take on events in France almost led to his dismissal.) Influenced by Thomas Paine's *The Rights of Man*, Burns's poem 'Is There for Honest Poverty' (1795) contains some of his most enduring sentiments on egalitarianism. In it he champions the man of 'independent mind' and lampoons the baubles associated with rank and station. Burns envisages a time when people will be judged on merit alone, creating both a national and international brotherhood. It's clear why this son of Alloway's message travelled successfully to regions like Soviet Russia, where Burns Night is still celebrated every 25th of January. The problem with Burns Night, however, is that it is often reductive. People swig their whisky and clap their hands as a piper marches into the room, followed by a chef carrying the platter groaning with haggis. The famed poem is recited, the haggis sliced open and then everyone tucks in. Tartan is worn or displayed, and there may be dancing or song. This gives only the most slender glimpse of Burns as a man and as a poet. Read a lyric such as 'Man Was Made to Mourn' and you begin to sense something close to melancholy. It talks of oppression and man's 'inhumanity', and pleads once more for equality and freedom. The 'independent mind' of 'Is There for Honest Poverty' here becomes 'an independent wish'. (As I write this Introduction, there are few in Scotland who can equate the word 'independent' with anything other than a sundering of the political union with England.) The simmering anger in these poems seems a world away from the 'couthy' sentiments expressed in 'Afton Water' or 'Farewell to the Highlands'. Burns, a lover of spirits and a spirited lover, was also afflicted by occasional depression and self-doubt.

It is hard to know how to reconcile these different facets of the poet's character, and I'm not convinced such toil needs to be undertaken. Burns, to steal Walt Whitman's phrase, 'contains multitudes'. He can be political, or intimately romantic. He can extol the virtues of nature, but also castigate the vagaries of human nature. Just as he charmed polite society in Edinburgh on his several visits, so he was every bit as comfortable among the regulars at the Globe Inn in Dumfries (to the point of scratching stanzas and aphorisms on its windows). We admire him for the breadth of his knowledge and artistry, for the wry humour and earthly passion exhibited in many of his poems and lyrics. We admire his humanism and belief in commonality. He showed the world that you could be a poet whatever your background and apparent station in life. He remains popular as well as populist and is a great user of the vernacular. Scots is a language ready-made for poetry, bringing with it a multitude of synonyms, images and onomatopoeic words, and 'Tam o' Shanter' remains the greatest poem in the Scots language – at least until Hugh MacDiarmid. It is a celebration of community (the 'drouthy neebors' of the opening lines, meaning 'thirsty friends'), but also of storytelling and linguistic verve. It takes delight in itself, which makes it a delight as a performance. It also pulls off a feat unique in poetry, in being humorous and frightening in near-equal measure.

It can be found, of course, in this selection of the best of Robert Burns's poems and songs.

Ian Rankin

O Once I Lov'd
(TUNE: I AM A MAN UNMARRIED (NOT EXTANT))

O once I lov'd a bonny lass
    Ay and I love her still
And whilst that virtue warms my breast
    I'll love my handsome Nell.
                Fal lal de dal &c.

As bonny lasses I hae seen,
    And mony full as braw;
But for a modest gracefu' mien,
    The like I never saw.

A bonny lass I will confess
    Is pleasant to the e'e;
But without some better qualities
    She's no a lass for me.

But Nelly's looks are blythe and sweet,
    And what is best of a',
Her reputation is compleat
    And fair without a flaw.

She dresses ay sae clean and neat,
    Both decent and genteel;
And then there's something in her gate
    Gars ony dress look weel.

A gaudy dress and gentle air
    May slightly touch the heart;
But it's innocence and modesty
    That polisses the dart.

'Tis this in Nelly pleases me;
    'Tis this inchants my soul;
For absolutely in my breast
    She reigns without controul.

Finis

Mary Morison
(TUNE: DUNCAN DAVISON)

O Mary, at thy window be,
    It is the wish'd, the trysted hour;
Those smiles and glances let me see,
    That make the miser's treasure poor:
How blythly wad I bide the stoure,
    A weary slave frae sun to sun;
Could I the rich reward secure,
    The lovely Mary Morison.

Yestreen when to the trembling string
    The dance gaed thro' the lighted ha',
To thee my fancy took its wing,
    I sat, but neither heard nor saw:
Tho' this was fair, and that was braw,
    And yon the toast of a' the town,
I sigh'd, and said amang them a',
    'Ye are na Mary Morison.'

O Mary, canst thou wreck his peace,
    Wha for thy sake wad gladly die!
Or canst thou break that heart of his,
    Whase only faut is loving thee.
If love for love thou wilt na gie,
    At least be pity to me shown;
A thought ungentle canna be
    The thought o' Mary Morison.

It Was Upon a Lammas Night
(TUNE: CORN RIGS ARE BONIE)

It was upon a Lammas night,
   When corn rigs are bonie,
Beneath the moon's unclouded light,
   I held awa to Annie:
The time flew by, wi' tentless heed,
   Till 'tween the late and early;
Wi' sma' persuasion she agreed,
   To see me thro' the barley.

The sky was blue, the wind was still,
   The moon was shining clearly;
I set her down, wi' right good will,
   Amang the rigs o' barley:
I ken't her heart was a' my ain;
   I lov'd her most sincerely;
I kiss'd her owre and owre again,
   Amang the rigs o' barley.

I lock'd her in my fond embrace;
   Her heart was beating rarely:
My blessings on that happy place,
   Amang the rigs o' barley!
But by the moon and stars so bright,
   That shone that hour so clearly!
She ay shall bless that happy night,
   Amang the rigs o' barley.

I hae been blythe wi' comrades dear;
   I hae been merry drinking;
I hae been joyfu' gath'rin gear;
   I hae been happy thinking;
But a' the pleasures e'er I saw,
   Tho' three times doubl'd fairly,
That happy night was worth them a',
   Amang the rigs o' barley.

Corn rigs, an' barley rigs,
   An' corn rigs are bonie:
I'll ne'er forget that happy night
   Amang the rigs wi' Annie.

Song Composed in August
(TUNES: I HAD A HORSE, I HAD NAE MAIR; PORT GORDON)

Now westlin winds, and slaught'ring guns
    Bring Autumn's pleasant weather;
And the moorcock springs, on whirring wings,
    Amang the blooming heather:
Now waving grain, wide o'er the plain,
    Delights the weary farmer;
And the moon shines bright, when I rove at night,
    To muse upon my charmer.

The partridge loves the fruitful fells;
    The plover loves the mountains;
The woodcock haunts the lonely dells;
    The soaring hern the fountains:
Thro' lofty groves, the cushat roves,
    The path of man to shun it;
The hazel bush o'erhangs the thrush,
    The spreading thorn the linnet.

Thus ev'ry kind their pleasure find,
    The savage and the tender;
Some social join, and leagues combine;
    Some solitary wander;
Avaunt, away! the cruel sway,
    Tyrannic man's dominion;
The sportsman's joy, the murd'ring cry,
    The flutt'ring, gory pinion!

But Peggy dear, the ev'ning's clear,
  Thick flies the skimming swallow;
The sky is blue, the fields in view,
  All fading-green and yellow:
Come let us stray our gladsome way,
  And view the charms of nature;
The rustling corn, the fruited thorn,
  And ev'ry happy creature.

We'll gently walk, and sweetly talk,
  Till the silent moon shine clearly;
I'll grasp thy waist, and fondly prest,
  Swear how I love thee dearly:
Not vernal show'rs to budding flow'rs,
  Not autumn to the farmer,
So dear can be, as thou to me,
  My fair, my lovely charmer!

John Barleycorn[*]
A Ballad
(TUNES: COLD AND RAW; LULL ME BEYOND THEE)

There was three kings into the east,
　　Three kings both great and high,
And they hae sworn a solemn oath
　　John Barleycorn should die.

They took a plough and plough'd him down,
　　Put clods upon his head,
And they hae sworn a solemn oath
　　John Barleycorn was dead.

But the chearful spring came kindly on,
　　And show'rs began to fall;
John Barleycorn got up again,
　　And sore surpris'd them all.

The sultry suns of summer came,
　　And he grew thick and strong,
His head weel arm'd wi' pointed spears,
　　That no one should him wrong.

The sober autumn enter'd mild,
　　When he grew wan and pale;
His bending joints and drooping head
　　Show'd he began to fail.

[*] This is partly composed on the plan of an old song known by the same name. [RB]

His colour sicken'd more and more,
    He faded into age;
And then his enemies began
    To show their deadly rage.

They've taen a weapon, long and sharp,
    And cut him by the knee;
Then ty'd him fast upon a cart,
    Like a rogue for forgerie.

They laid him down upon his back,
    And cudgell'd him full sore;
They hung him up before the storm,
    And turn'd him o'er and o'er.

They filled up a darksome pit
    With water to the brim,
They heaved in John Barleycorn,
    There let him sink or swim.

They laid him out upon the floor,
    To work him farther woe,
And still, as signs of life appear'd,
    They toss'd him to and fro.

They wasted, o'er a scorching flame,
    The marrow of his bones;
But a miller us'd him worst of all,
    For he crush'd him between two stones.

And they hae taen his very heart's blood,
    And drank it round and round;
And still the more and more they drank,
    Their joy did more abound.

John Barleycorn was a hero bold,
    Of noble enterprise,
For if you do but taste his blood,
    'Twill make your courage rise.

'Twill make a man forget his woe;
    'Twill heighten all his joy:
'Twill make the widow's heart to sing,
    Tho' the tear were in her eye.

Then let us toast John Barleycorn,
    Each man a glass in hand;
And may his great posterity
    Ne'er fail in old Scotland!

Poor Mailie's Elegy

Lament in rhyme, lament in prose,
Wi' saut tears trickling down your nose;
Our *Bardie's* fate is at a close,
   Past a' remead!
The last, sad cape-stane of his woes;
   Poor Mailie's dead!

It's no the loss o' warl's gear,
That could sae bitter draw the tear,
Or make our *Bardie*, dowie, wear
   The mourning weed:
He's lost a friend and neebor dear,
   In *Mailie* dead.

Thro' a' the town she trotted by him;
A lang half-mile she could descry him;
Wi' kindly bleat, when she did spy him,
   She ran wi' speed:
A friend mair faithfu' ne'er came nigh him,
   Than *Mailie* dead.

I wat she was a *sheep* o' sense,
An could behave hersel wi' mense:
I'll say't, she never brak a fence,
   Thro' thievish greed.
Our *Bardie*, lanely, keeps the spence
   Sin' *Mailie's* dead.

Or, if he wanders up the howe,
Her living image in *her yowe*,
Comes bleating till him, owre the knowe,
       For bits o' bread;
An' down the briny pearls rowe
       For *Mailie* dead.

She was nae get o' moorlan tips,
Wi' tauted ket, an' hairy hips;
For her forbears were brought in ships,
       Frae 'yont the Tweed:
A bonier *fleesh* ne'er cross'd the clips
       Than *Mailie's* dead.

Wae worth that man wha first did shape,
That vile, wanchancie thing – *a raep*!
It maks guid fellows girn an' gape,
       Wi' chokin dread;
An' *Robin's* bonnet wave wi' crape
       For *Mailie* dead.

O, a' ye *Bards* on bonie Doon!
An' wha on Aire your chanters tune!
Come, join the melancholious croon
       O' *Robin's* reed!
His heart will never get aboon!
       His *Mailie's* dead!

My Father Was a Farmer
(TUNE: THE WEAVER AND HIS SHUTTLE, O)

My father was a farmer upon the Carrick border, O
And carefully he bred me in decency and order, O
He bade me act a manly part, though I had ne'er a
    farthing, O
For without an honest manly heart, no man was worth
    regarding, O.

Then out into the world my course I did determine, O
Tho' to be rich was not my wish, yet to be great was
    charming, O
My talents they were not the worst; nor yet my
    education, O
Resolv'd was I, at least to try, to mend my situation, O.

In many a way, and vain essay, I courted fortune's favor, O
Some cause unseen still stept between to frustrate each
    endeavour, O
Sometimes by foes I was o'erpower'd; sometimes by
    friends forsaken, O
And when my hope was at the top, I still was worst
    mistaken, O.

Then sore harass'd, and tir'd at last, with fortune's vain
    delusion, O
I dropt my schemes, like idle dreams, and came to this
    conclusion, O
The past was bad, the future hid; its good or ill untryed, O
But the present hour was in my pow'r, and so I would
    enjoy it, O.

No help, nor hope, nor view had I; nor person to
    befriend me, O
So I must toil, and sweat and moil, and labor to sustain
    me, O
To plough and sow, to reap and mow, my father bred
    me early, O
For one, he said, to labor bred, was a match for fortune
    fairly, O.

Thus all obscure, unknown, and poor, thro' life I'm
    doom'd to wander, O
Till down my weary bones I lay in everlasting slumber,
    O
No view nor care, but shun whate'er might breed me
    pain or sorrow, O
I live today, as well's I may, regardless of tomorrow, O.

But cheerful still, I am as well, as a monarch in a
    palace, O
Tho' fortune's frown still hunts me down, with all her
    wonted malice, O
I make indeed, my daily bread, but ne'er can make it
    farther, O
But as daily bread is all I need, I do not much regard
    her, O.

When sometimes by my labor I earn a little money, O
Some unforseen misfortune comes generally upon me,
    O
Mischance, mistake, or by neglect, or my good-natur'd
    folly, O
But come what will, I've sworn it still, I'll ne'er be
    melancholy, O.

All you who follow wealth and power with unremitting
   ardor, O
The more in this you look for bliss, you leave your view
   the farther, O
Had you the wealth Potosi boasts, or nations to adore
   you, O
A cheerful honest-hearted clown I will prefer before
   you, O.

Green Grow the Rashes. A Fragment
(TUNE: GREEN GROWS THE RASHES)

CHORUS

Green grow the rashes, O;
Green grow the rashes, O;
The sweetest hours that e'er I spend,
   Are spent amang the lasses, O.

There's nought but care on ev'ry han',
   In ev'ry hour that passes, O:
What signifies the life o' man,
   An' 'twere na for the lasses, O?
         Green grow, &c.

The warly race may riches chase,
   An' riches still may fly them, O;
An' tho' at last they catch them fast,
   Their hearts can ne'er enjoy them, O.
         Green grow, &c.

But gie me a canny hour at e'en,
   My arms about my Dearie, O;
An' warly cares, an' warly men,
   May a' gae tapsalteerie, O!
         Green grow, &c.

For you sae douse, ye sneer at this,
   Ye're nought but senseless asses, O:
The wisest Man the warl' saw,
   He dearly lov'd the lasses, O.
         Green grow, &c.

Auld Nature swears, the lovely Dears
Her noblest work she classes, O:
Her prentice han' she try'd on man,
An' then she made the lasses, O.
Green grow, &c.

Holy Willie's Prayer

'And send the Godly in a pet to pray –' Pope

O Thou, wha in the heavens dost dwell,
Wha, as it pleases best thysel',
Sends ane to heaven and ten to hell,
   A' for thy glory,
And no for ony guid or ill
    They've done afore thee!

I bless and praise thy matchless might,
Whan thousands thou hast left in night,
That I am here afore thy sight,
   For gifts an' grace,
A burnin' an' a shinin' light,
    To a' this place.

What was I, or my generation,
That I should get such exaltation,
I wha deserve sic just damnation,
   For broken laws,
Five thousand years ere my creation,
    Thro' Adam's cause.

When frae my mither's womb I fell,
Thou might ha'e plunged me in hell,
To gnash my gums, to weep and wail,
   In burnin' lake,
Whar damned devils roar and yell,
    Chain'd to a stake.

Yet I am here a chosen sample,
To show thy grace is great an' ample;
I'm here a pillar in thy temple,
        Strong as a rock,
A guide, a buckler, an' example
        To a' thy flock.

But yet, O Lord! confess I must,
At times I'm fash'd wi' fleshly lust
An' sometimes too, wi' warldly trust,
        Vile Self gets in;
But thou remembers we are dust,
        Defil'd in sin.

O Lord! yestreen, thou kens, wi' Meg –
Thy pardon I sincerely beg –
O may't ne'er be a living plague
        To my dishonor!
An' I'll ne'er lift a lawless leg
        Again upon her.

Besides, I farther maun avow –
Wi' Leezie's lass, three times, I trow –
But, Lord, that Friday I was fou,
        When I cam near her,
Or else, thou kens, thy servant true
        Wad never steer her.

Maybe thou lets this fleshly thorn
Buffet thy servant e'en and morn,
Lest he owre proud and high should turn
        That he's sae gifted:
If sae, thy han' maun e'en be borne
        Until thou lift it.

Lord, bless thy Chosen in this place,
For here thou has a chosen race!
But God confound their stubborn face
           An' blast their name,
Wha bring thy elders to disgrace
           An' open shame!

Lord mind Gaun Hamilton's deserts,
He drinks, an' swears, an' plays at carts,
Yet has sae mony takin' arts,
           Wi' great an' sma'
Frae God's ain priest the people's hearts
           He steals awa'.

An' whan we chasten'd him therefore,
Thou kens how he bred sic a splore,
As set the warld in a roar
           O laughin' at us;
Curse thou his basket and his store,
           Kail an' potatoes.

Lord hear my earnest cry an' pray'r
Against that presbyt'ry o' Ayr;
Thy strong right hand, Lord make it bare,
           Upo' their heads,
Lord weigh it down, and dinna spare,
           For their misdeeds.

O Lord my God, that glib-tongu'd Aiken,
My very heart an' soul are quakin',
To think how we stood, sweatin', shakin',
           An' pissed wi' dread,
While Auld wi' hingin lip gaed sneakin',
           And hid his head.

Lord in the day of vengeance try him,
Lord visit them wha did employ him,
And pass not in thy mercy by 'em,
                    Nor hear their prayer;
But for thy people's sake destroy 'em,
                    And dinna spare.

But Lord remember me and mine
Wi' mercies temp'ral and divine,
That I for gear and grace may shine,
                    Excell'd by nane,
An' a' the glory shall be thine,
                    Amen, Amen.

A Poet's Welcome to His Love-Begotten Daughter; The First Instance that Entitled Him to the Venerable Appellation of Father

Thou's welcome wean, mischanter fa' me,
If thoughts o' thee, or yet thy Mamie,
Shall ever daunton me, or awe me,
       My sweet wee lady,
Or if I blush when thou shalt ca' me
       Tit-ta or daddy.

What tho' they ca' me fornicator,
An' tease my name in kintry clatter:
The mair they tauk I'm kent the better,
       E'en let them clash;
An auld wife's tongue's a feckless matter
       To gie ane fash.

Welcome, my bonie, sweet, wee dochter!
Tho' ye come here a wee unsought for,
And tho' your comin I hae fought for
       Baith kirk and queir;
Yet, by my faith, ye're no unwrought for –
       That I shall swear!

Wee image of my bonny Betty,
I fatherly will kiss and daut thee,
As dear an' near my heart I set thee
       Wi' as gude will
As a' the priests had seen me get thee
       That's out o' hell.

Sweet fruit o' mony a merry dint,
My funny toil is no a' tint;
Tho' ye came to the warl asklent,
                    Which fools may scoff at;
In my last plack thy part's be in't,
                    The better ha'f o't.

Tho' I should be the waur bestead,
Thou's be as braw and bienly clad,
And thy young years as nicely bred
                    Wi' education,
As onie brat o' wedlock's bed
                    In a' thy station.

Gude grant that thou may ay inherit
Thy mither's looks, and gracefu' merit;
An' thy poor worthless dady's spirit,
                    Without his failins,
'Twill please me mair to see thee heir it
                    Than stocket mailens.

An' if thou be what I wad ha'e thee,
An' tak the counsel I sall gi'e thee,
A lovin' father I'll be to thee,
                    If thou be spar'd;
Thro' a' thy childish years I'll e'e thee,
                    An' think't weel war'd.

The Fornicator. A New Song
(TUNE: CLOUT THE CALDRON)

Ye jovial boys who love the joys,
    The blissful joys of lovers;
Yet dare avow with dauntless brow,
    When th' bonie lass discovers;
I pray draw near and lend an ear,
    And welcome in a frater,
For I've lately been on quarantine,
    A proven Fornicator.

Before the congregation wide
    I pass'd the muster fairly,
My handsome Betsey by my side,
    We gat our ditty rarely;
But my downcast eye by chance did spy
    What made my lips to water,
Those limbs so clean where I, between,
    Commenc'd a Fornicator.

With rueful face and signs of grace
    I pay'd the buttock-hire,
The night was dark and thro' the park
    I could not but convoy her;
A parting kiss, what could I less,
    My vows began to scatter,
My Betsey fell – lal de dal lal lal,
    I am a Fornicator.

But for her sake this vow I make,
    And solemnly I swear it,
That while I own a single crown,
    She's welcome for to share it;
And my roguish boy his mother's joy,
    And the darling of his pater,
For him I boast my pains and cost,
    Although a Fornicator.

Ye wenching blades whose hireling jades
    Have tipt you off blue-boram,
I tell ye plain, I do disdain
    To rank you in the quorum;
But a bonie lass upon the grass
    To teach her *esse mater*;
And no reward but for regard,
    O that's a Fornicator.

Your warlike kings and heroes bold,
    Great captains and commanders;
Your mighty Cèsars fam'd of old,
    And conquering Alexanders;
In fields they fought and laurels bought
    And bulwarks strong did batter,
And still they grac'd our noble list
    And ranked Fornicator!

On Burns' Horse Being Impounded

Was e'er puir Poet sae befitted,
The maister drunk – the horse committed:
Puir harmless beast! Tak' thee nae care,
Thou'lt be a horse when he's nae mair.

Man Was Made to Mourn. A Dirge
(TUNE: PEGGY BAWN)

When chill November's surly blast
   Made fields and forests bare,
One ev'ning, as I wander'd forth,
   Along the banks of Aire,
I spy'd a man, whose aged step
   Seem'd weary, worn with care;
His face was furrow'd o'er with years,
   And hoary was his hair.

Young stranger, whither wand'rest thou?
   Began the rev'rend Sage;
Does thirst of wealth thy step constrain,
   Or youthful pleasure's rage?
Or haply, prest with cares and woes,
   Too soon thou hast began,
To wander forth, with me, to mourn
   The miseries of Man.

The sun that overhangs yon moors,
   Out-spreading far and wide,
Where hundreds labour to support
   A haughty lordling's pride;
I've seen yon weary winter-sun
   Twice forty times return;
And ev'ry time has added proofs,
   That Man was made to mourn.

O Man! while in thy early years,
    How prodigal of time!
Mispending all thy precious hours,
    Thy glorious, youthful prime!
Alternate follies take the sway;
    Licentious passions burn;
Which tenfold force gives Nature's law,
    That Man was made to mourn.

Look not alone on youthful prime,
    Or manhood's active might;
Man then is useful to his kind,
    Supported is his right:
But see him on the edge of life,
    With cares and sorrows worn,
Then age and want, Oh! ill-match'd pair!
    Show Man was made to mourn.

A few seem favourites of Fate,
    In pleasure's lap carest;
Yet think not all the Rich and Great,
    Are likewise truly blest.
But Oh! what crouds in ev'ry land,
    All wretched and forlorn,
Thro' weary life this lesson learn,
    That Man was made to mourn!

Many and sharp the num'rous ills
    Inwoven with our frame!
More pointed still we make ourselves,
    Regret, remorse and shame!

And Man, whose heav'n-erected face,
    The smiles of love adorn,
Man's inhumanity to Man
    Makes countless thousands mourn!

See yonder poor, o'erlabour'd wight,
    So abject, mean and vile,
Who begs a brother of the earth
    To give him leave to toil;
And see his lordly *fellow-worm*,
    The poor petition spurn,
Unmindful, tho' a weeping wife,
    And helpless offspring mourn.

If I'm design'd yon lordling's slave,
    By Nature's law design'd,
Why was an independent wish
    E'er planted in my mind?
If not, why am I subject to
    His cruelty, or scorn?
Or why has Man the will and pow'r
    To make his fellow mourn?

Yet let not this too much, my son,
    Disturb thy youthful breast:
This partial view of human-kind
    Is surely not the *last*!
The poor, oppressed, honest man
    Had never, sure, been born,
Had there not been some recompense
    To comfort those that mourn!

O Death! the poor man's dearest friend,
    The kindest and the best!
Welcome the hour, my aged limbs
    Are laid with thee at rest!
The great, the wealthy fear thy blow,
    From pomp and pleasure torn;
But Oh! a blest relief for those
    That weary-laden mourn!

The Holy Fair

A robe of seeming truth and trust
Hid crafty observation;
And secret hung, with poison'd crust,
The dirk of defamation:
A mask that like the gorget show'd,
Dye-varying, on the pigeon;
And for a mantle large and broad,
He wrapt him in Religion.

Hypocrisy a-la-Mode

Upon a simmer Sunday morn,
    When Nature's face is fair,
I walked forth to view the corn,
    And snuff the callor air.
The rising sun, owre Galston muirs,
    Wi' glorious light was glintan;
The hares were hirplan down the furrs,
    The lav'rocks they were chantan
                    Fu' sweet that day.

As lightsomely I glowr'd abroad,
    To see a scene sae gay,
Three hizzies, early at the road,
    Cam skelpan up the way.
Twa had manteeles o' dolefu' black,
    But ane wi' lyart lining;
The third, that gaed a wee a-back,
    Was in the fashion shining
                    Fu' gay that day.

The *twa* appear'd like sisters twin,
    In feature, form an' claes;
Their visage wither'd, lang an' thin,
    As sour as ony slaes:
The *third* cam up, hap-step-an'-loup,
    As light as ony lambie,
An' wi' a curchie low did stoop,
    As soon as e'er she saw me,
                    Fu' kind that day.

Wi' bonnet aff, quoth I, 'Sweet lass,
    I think ye seem to ken me;
I'm sure I've seen that bonie face,
    But yet I canna name ye.'
Quo' she, an laughan as she spak,
    An' taks me by the han's,
'Ye, for my sake, hae gien the feck
    Of a' the *ten comman*'s
                    A screed some day.

'My name is Fun – your cronie dear,
    The nearest friend ye hae;
An' this is Superstition here,
    An' that's Hypocrisy.
I'm gaun to Mauchline *holy fair*,
    To spend an hour in daffin:
Gin ye go there, yon runkl'd pair,
    We will get famous laughin
                    At them this day.'

Quoth I, 'With a' my heart I'll do't;
    I'll get my Sunday's sark on,
An' meet you on the holy spot;
    Faith, we'se hae fine remarkin!'

Then I gaed hame at crowdie-time,
    An' soon I made me ready;
For roads were clad, frae side to side,
    Wi' monie a wearie body,
                In droves that day.

Here, farmers gash, in ridin graith,
    Gaed hoddan by their cotters;
There, swankies young, in braw braid-claith,
    Are springan owre the gutters.
The lasses, skelpan barefit, thrang,
    In silks and scarlets glitter;
Wi' *sweet-milk cheese*, in many a whang,
    An' *farls*, bak'd wi' butter,
                Fu' crump that day.

When by the *plate* we set our nose,
    Weel heaped up wi' ha'pence,
A greedy glowr *black-bonnet* throws,
    An' we maun draw our tippence.
Then in we go to see the show,
    On ev'ry side they're gath'ran;
Some carryan dails, some chairs an' stools,
    An' some are busy bleth'ran
                Right loud that day.

Here stands a shed to fend the show'rs,
    An' screen our countra gentry;
There *racer Jess*, an' twathree wh-res,
    Are blinkan at the entry.
Here sits a raw o' tittlan jads,
    Wi' heaving breasts an' bare neck;
And there a batch o' Wabster lads,
    Blackguarding from Kilmarnock
                For *fun* this day.

Here, some are thinkan on their sins,
    An' some upo' their claes;
Ane curses feet that fyl'd his shins,
    Anither sighs an' prays:
On this hand sits an *Elect* swatch,
    Wi' screw'd-up, grace-proud faces;
On that, a set o' chaps, at watch,
    Thrang winkan on the lasses
                    To *chairs* that day.

O happy is that man, an' blest!
    Nae wonder that it pride him!
Whase ain dear lass, that he likes best,
    Comes clinkan down beside him!
Wi' arm repos'd on the *chair-back*,
    He sweetly does compose him;
Which, by degrees, slips round her *neck*
    An's loof upon her *bosom*
                    Unkend that day.

Now a' the congregation o'er
    Is silent expectation;
For Sawney speels the holy door,
    Wi' tidings of salvation.
Should *Hornie*, as in ancient days,
    'Mang sons o' God present him,
The vera sight o' Moodie's face,
    To's ain *het hame* had sent him
                    Wi' fright that day.

Hear how he clears the points o' faith
    Wi' rattlin an' thumpin!
Now meekly calm, now wild in wrath,
    He's stampan, an he's jumpan!

His lengthen'd chin, his turn'd up snout,
  His eldritch squeel an' gestures,
O how they fire the heart devout,
  Like *cantharidian* plaisters
              On sic a day!

But hark! the *tent* has chang'd its voice;
  There's peace an' rest nae langer;
For a' the *real judges* rise,
  They canna sit for anger.
Smith opens out his cauld harangues,
  On *practice* and on *morals*;
An' aff the *godly* pour in thrangs,
  To gie the jars an' barrels
              A lift that day.

What signifies his barren shine,
  Of *moral pow'rs* an' *reason*?
His English style, an' gesture fine,
  Are a' clean out o' season.
Like Socrates or Antonine,
  Or some auld pagan heathen,
The *moral man* he does define,
  But ne'er a word o' *faith* in
              That's right this day.

In guid time comes an antidote
  Against sic poosion'd nostrum;
For Peebles, frae the water-fit,
  Ascends the *holy rostrum:*
See, up he's got the word o' God,
  An' meek an' mim has view'd it,
While Common Sense has taen the road,
  An' aff, an' up the Cowgate
              Fast, fast this day.

Wee Miller neist, the guard relieves,
  An' Orthodoxy raibles,
Tho' in his heart he weel believes,
  An' thinks it auld wives' fables:
But faith! the birkie wants a *Manse*,
  So, cannilie he hums them;
Altho' his carnal Wit an' Sense
  Like hafflins-wise o'ercomes him
          At times that day.

Now, butt an' ben, the change-house fills,
  Wi' yill-caup Commentators:
Here's crying out for bakes an' gills,
  An' there the pint-stowp clatters;
While thick an' thrang, an' loud an' lang,
  Wi' *Logic*, an' wi' *Scripture*,
They raise a din that in the end,
  Is like to breed a rupture
          O' wrath that day.

Leeze me on Drink! it gies us mair
  Than either school or colledge:
It kindles wit, it waukens lear,
  It pangs us fou o' knowledge.
Be't *whisky-gill* or *penny-wheep*,
  Or ony stronger potion,
It never fails, on drinkin deep,
  To kittle up our *notion*,
          By night or day.

The lads and lasses, blythely bent
  To mind baith *saul* an' *body*,
Sit round the table, weel content,
  An' steer about the *toddy*.

On this ane's dress, an' that ane's leuk,
   They're makin observations;
While some are cozie i' the neuk,
   An' forming *assignations*
               To meet some day.

But now the Lord's ain trumpet touts,
   Till a' the hills are rairan,
An' echos back return the shouts;
   Black Russel is na spairan:
His piercin words, like Highlan swords,
   Divide the joints an' marrow;
His talk o' Hell, where devils dwell,
   Our vera *'sauls does harrow'
              Wi' fright that day!

A vast, unbottom'd, boundless *Pit*,
   Fill'd fou o' *lowan brunstane*,
Whase raging flame, an' scorching heat,
   Wad melt the hardest whun-stane!
The *half asleep* start up wi' fear,
   An' think they hear it roaran,
When presently it does appear,
   'Twas but some neebor *snoran*
             Asleep that day.

'Twad be owre lang a tale to tell,
   How monie stories past,
An' how they crouded to the yill,
   When they were a' dismist:
How drink gaed round, in cogs an' caups,
   Amang the furms an' benches;

---

* Shakespeare's Hamlet. [RB]

An' cheese an' bread, frae women's laps,
　　Was dealt about in lunches,
　　　　　　An' dawds that day.

In comes a gawsie, gash Guidwife,
　　An' sits down by the fire,
Syne draws her *kebbuck* an' her knife;
　　The lasses they are shyer.
The auld Guidmen, about the *grace*,
　　Frae side to side they bother,
Till some ane by his bonnet lays,
　　And gies them't, like a *tether*,
　　　　　　Fu' lang that day.

Waesucks! for him that gets nae lass,
　　Or lasses that hae naething!
Sma' need has he to say a grace,
　　Or melvie his braw claithing!
O Wives be mindfu', ance yourself,
　　How bonie lads ye wanted,
An' dinna, for a *kebbuck-heel*,
　　Let lasses be affronted
　　　　　　On sic a day!

Now Clinkumbell, wi' rattlan tow,
　　Begins to jow an' croon;
Some swagger hame, the best they dow,
　　Some wait the afternoon.
At slaps the billies halt a blink,
　　Till lasses strip their shoon:
Wi' *faith* an' *hope*, an' *love* an' *drink*,
　　They're a' in famous tune
　　　　　　For crack that day.

How monie hearts this day converts,
    O' sinners and o' lasses!
Their hearts o' stane, gin night are gane,
    As saft as ony flesh is.
There's some are fou o' *love divine*;
    There's some are fou o' *brandy*;
An' monie jobs that day begin,
    May end in *Houghmagandie*
                Some ither day.

To a Mouse
On Turning Her up in Her Nest with the Plough, November 1785

Wee, sleeket, cowran, tim'rous *beastie*,
O, what a panic's in thy breastie!
Thou need na start awa sae hasty,
            Wi' bickering brattle!
I wad be laith to rin an' chase thee,
            Wi' murd'ring *pattle*!

I'm truly sorry Man's dominion
Has broken Nature's social union,
An' justifies that ill opinion,
            Which makes thee startle,
At me, thy poor, earth-born companion,
            An' *fellow-mortal*!

I doubt na, whyles, but thou may thieve;
What then? poor beastie, thou maun live!
A *daimen-icker* in a *thrave*
            'S a sma' request:
I'll get a blessin wi' the lave,
            An' never miss't!

Thy wee-bit *housie*, too, in ruin!
It's silly wa's the win's are strewin!
An' naething, now, to big a new ane,
            O' foggage green!
An' bleak December's winds ensuin,
            Baith snell an' keen!

Thou saw the fields laid bare an' wast,
An' weary Winter comin fast,
An' cozie here, beneath the blast,
                    Thou thought to dwell,
Till crash! the cruel *coulter* past
                    Out thro' thy cell.

That wee-bit heap o' leaves an' stibble,
Has cost thee monie a weary nibble!
Now thou's turn'd out, for a' thy trouble,
                    But house or hald,
To thole the Winter's sleety dribble,
                    An' *cranreuch* cauld!

But Mousie, thou art no thy-lane,
In proving *foresight* may be vain:
The best laid schemes o' *Mice* an' *Men*,
                    Gang aft agley,
An' lea'e us nought but grief an' pain,
                    For promis'd joy!

Still, thou art blest, compar'd wi' *me*!
The *present* only toucheth thee:
But Och! I *backward* cast my e'e,
                    On prospects drear!
An' *forward*, tho' I canna *see*,
                    I *guess* an' *fear*!

To a Louse
On Seeing One on a Lady's Bonnet at Church

Ha! whare ye gaun, ye crowlan ferlie!
Your impudence protects you sairly:
I canna say but ye strunt rarely,
        Owre *gawze* and *lace;*
Tho' faith, I fear ye dine but sparely,
        On sic a place.

Ye ugly, creepan, blastet wonner,
Detested, shunn'd, by saunt an' sinner,
How daur ye set your fit upon her,
        Sae fine a *Lady!*
Gae somewhere else and seek your dinner,
        On some poor body.

Swith, in some beggar's haffet squattle;
There ye may creep, and sprawl, and sprattle,
Wi' ither kindred, jumping cattle,
        In shoals and nations;
Whare *horn* nor *bane* ne'er daur unsettle,
        Your thick plantations.

Now haud you there, ye're out o' sight,
Below the fatt'rels, snug and tight,
Na faith ye yet! ye'll no be right,
        Till ye've got on it,
The vera tapmost, towrin height
        O' *Miss's bonnet.*

My sooth! right bauld ye set your nose out,
As plump an' gray as onie grozet:
O for some rank, mercurial rozet,
                    Or fell, red smeddum,
I'd gie you sic a hearty dose o't,
                    Wad dress your droddum!

I wad na been surpriz'd to spy
You on an auld wife's *flainen toy*;
Or aiblins some bit duddie boy,
                    On's *wylecoat*;
But Miss's fine *Lunardi*, fye!
                    How daur ye do't?

O *Jenny* dinna toss your head,
An' set your beauties a' abread!
Ye little ken what cursed speed
                    The blastie's makin,
Thae *winks* and *finger-ends*, I dread,
                    Are notice takin!

O wad some Pow'r the giftie gie us
To see oursels as others see us!
It wad frae monie a blunder free us
                    An' foolish notion:
What airs in dress an' gait wad lea'e us,
                    And ev'n Devotion!

The Author's Earnest Cry and Prayer,* to the Right Honorable and Honorable, the Scotch Representatives in the House of Commons

> Dearest of Distillations last and best! –
> How art thou lost! –
>
>   Parody on Milton

Ye Irish lords, ye knights an' squires,
Wha represent our Brughs an' Shires
An' dousely manage our affairs
                    In Parliament,
To you a simple Bardie's pray'rs
                    Are humbly sent.

Alas! my roupet Muse is haerse!
Your Honor's hearts wi' grief 'twad pierce,
To see her sittan on her arse
                    Low i' the dust,
An' scriechan out prosaic verse,
                    An' like to brust!

Tell them wha hae the chief direction,
Scotland an' *me's* in great affliction,
E'er sin' they laid that curst restriction
                    On Aquavitae;
An' rouse them up to strong conviction,
                    An' move their pity.

---

* This was wrote before the Act anent the Scotch distilleries, of session 1786; for which Scotland and the Author return their most grateful thanks. [RB]

Stand forth and tell yon Premier Youth,
The honest, open, naked truth:
Tell him o' mine an' Scotland's drouth,
         His servants humble:
The muckle devil blaw you south,
         If ye dissemble!

Does ony *great man* glunch an' gloom?
Speak out an' never fash your thumb.
Let *posts* an' *pensions* sink or swoom
         Wi' them wha grant them:
If honestly they canna come,
         Far better want them.

In gath'rin votes you were na slack,
Now stand as tightly by your tack:
Ne'er claw your lug, an' fidge your back,
         An' hum an' haw,
But raise your arm, an' tell your crack
         Before them a'.

Paint Scotland greetan owre her thrissle;
Her *mutchkin stowp* as toom's a whissle;
An' damn'd Excise-men in a bussle,
         Seizan a *Stell*,
Triumphant crushan't like a muscle
         Or laimpet shell.

Then on the tither hand present her,
A blackguard *Smuggler*, right behint her,
An' cheek-for-chow, a chuffie *Vintner*,
         Colleaguing join,
Picking her pouch as bare as Winter,
         Of a' kind coin.

Is there, that bears the name o' Scot,
But feels his heart's bluid rising hot,
To see his poor, auld Mither's *pot*,
                    Thus dung in staves,
An' plunder'd o' her hindmost groat,
                    By gallows knaves?

Alas! I'm but a nameless wight,
Trode i' the mire out o' sight!
But could I like Montgomeries fight,
                    Or gab like Boswell,
There's some *sark-necks* I wad *draw* tight,
                    An' *tye* some *hose* well.

God bless your Honors, can ye see't,
The kind, auld, cantie Carlin greet,
An' no get warmly to your feet,
                    An' gar them hear it,
An' tell them, with a patriot-heat,
                    Ye winna bear it?

Some o' you nicely ken the laws,
To round the period an' pause,
And with rhetoric clause on clause
                    To mak harangues;
Then echo thro' Saint Stephens wa's
                    Auld Scotland's wrangs.

Dempster, a true-blue Scot I'se warran;
Thee, aith-detesting, chaste Kilkerran;
An' that glib-gabbet Highland Baron,
                    The Laird o' Graham;
And ane, a chap that's damn'd auldfarran,
                    Dundas his name.

Erskine, a spunkie norland billie;
True Campbells, Frederick an' Ilay;
An' Liviston, the bauld Sir Willie;
              An' monie ithers,
Whom auld Demosthenes or Tully
                  Might own for brithers.

Arouse my boys! exert your mettle,
To get auld Scotland back her *kettle*!
Or faith! I'll wad my new pleugh-pettle,
              Ye'll see't or lang,
She'll teach you, wi' a reekan whittle,
                  Anither sang.

This while she's been in crankous mood,
Her *lost Militia* fir'd her bluid;
(Deil na they never mair do guid,
              Play'd her that pliskie!)
An' now she's like to rin red-wud
                  About her *Whisky*.

An' Lord! if ance they pit her till't,
Her tartan petticoat she'll kilt,
An' durk an' pistol at her belt,
              She'll tak the streets,
An' rin her whittle to the hilt,
                I' th' first she meets!

For God-sake, Sirs! then speak her fair,
An' straik her cannie wi' the hair,
An' to the *muckle house* repair,
              Wi' instant speed,
An' strive, wi' a' your Wit an' Lear,
                To get remead.

You ill-tongu'd tinkler, Charlie Fox,
May taunt you wi' his jeers an' mocks;
But gie him't het, my hearty cocks!
           E'en cowe the cadie!
An' send him to his dicing box,
           An' sportin lady.

Tell yon guid bluid o' auld Boconnock's,
I'll be his debt twa mashlum bonnocks,
An' drink his health in auld *Nanse Tinnock's
           Nine times a week,
If he some scheme, like tea an' winnocks,
           Wad kindly seek.

Could he some *commutation* broach,
I'll pledge my aith in guid braid Scotch,
He need na fear their foul reproach
           Nor erudition,
You mixtie-maxtie, queer hotch-potch,
           The *Coalition*.

Auld Scotland has a raucle tongue;
She's just a devil wi' a rung;
An' if she promise auld or young
           To tak their part,
Tho' by the neck she should be strung,
           She'll no desert.

And now, ye chosen Five and Forty,
May still your Mither's heart support ye;
Then, tho' a *Minister* grow dorty,

---

* A worthy old Hostess of the Author's in Mauchline, where he sometimes
studies Politics over a glass of guid auld Scotch Drink. [RB]

        An' kick your place,
Ye'll snap your fingers, poor an' hearty,
        Before his face.

God bless your Honors, a' your days,
Wi' sowps o' kail and brats o' claise,
In spite o' a' the thievish kaes
        That haunt St *Jamie*'s!
Your humble Bardie sings an' prays
        While *Rab* his name is.

POSTSCRIPT

Let half-starv'd slaves in warmer skies,
See future wines, rich-clust'ring, rise;
Their lot auld Scotland ne'er envies,
        But blythe an' frisky,
She eyes her freeborn, martial boys,
        Tak aff their Whisky.

What tho' their Phoebus kinder warms,
While Fragrance blooms an' Beauty charms!
When wretches range, in famish'd swarms,
        The scented groves,
Or hounded forth, *dishonor* arms
        In hungry droves.

Their *gun's* a burden on their shouther;
They downa bide the stink o' *powther*;
Their bauldest thought's a hank'ring swither,
        To stan' or rin,
Till skelp – a shot – they're aff, a' throw'ther,
        To save their skin.

But bring a Scotchman frae his hill,
Clap in his cheek a *Highland gill*,
Say, such is Royal George's will,
                    An' there's the foe,
He has nae thought but how to kill
                    Twa at a blow.

No cauld, faint-hearted doubtings tease him;
Death comes, wi' fearless eye he sees him;
Wi' bluidy han' a welcome gies him;
                    An' when he fa's,
His latest draught o' breathin lea'es him
                    In faint huzzas.

Sages their solemn een may steek,
An' raise a philosophic reek,
An' physically causes seek,
                    In *clime* an' *season*,
But tell me *Whisky's* name in Greek,
                    I'll tell the reason.

Scotland, my auld, respected Mither!
Tho' whyles ye moistify your leather,
Till whare ye sit, on craps o' heather,
                    Ye tine your dam;
FREEDOM and WHISKY gang thegither,
                    Tak aff your *dram*!

Scotch Drink

Gie him strong Drink until he wink.
That's sinking in despair;
And liquor *guid to fire his bluid,*
That's prest wi' grief an' care;
There let him bowse an' deep carouse.
Wi' bumpers flowing o'er.
Till he forgets his loves *or debts,*
An' minds his griefs no more.

Solomon's Proverbs, xxxi. 6, 7

Let other Poets raise a fracas
'Bout vines, an' wines, an' druken *Bacchus*,
An' crabbed names an' stories wrack us,
⠀⠀⠀⠀⠀⠀⠀An' grate our lug,
I sing the juice *Scotch bear* can mak us,
⠀⠀⠀⠀⠀⠀⠀In glass or jug.

O thou, my Muse! guid, auld Scotch Drink!
Whether thro' wimplin worms thou jink,
Or richly brown, ream owre the brink,
⠀⠀⠀⠀⠀⠀⠀In glorious faem,
Inspire me, till I *lisp* an' *wink*,
⠀⠀⠀⠀⠀⠀⠀To sing thy name!

Let husky Wheat the haughs adorn,
And Aits set up their awnie horn,
An' Pease an' Beans, at e'en or morn,
⠀⠀⠀⠀⠀⠀⠀Perfume the plain,
Leeze me on thee *John Barleycorn*,
⠀⠀⠀⠀⠀⠀⠀Thou king o' grain!

51

On thee aft Scotland chows her cood,
In souple scones, the wale o' food!
Or tumbling in the boiling flood
   Wi' kail an' beef;
But when thou pours thy strong *heart's blood*,
   There thou shines chief.

Food fills the wame, an' keeps us livin;
Tho' life's a gift no worth receivin,
When heavy-dragg'd wi' pine an' grievin;
   But oil'd by thee,
The wheels o' life gae down-hill, scrievin,
   Wi' rattlin glee.

Thou clears the head o' doited Lear,
Thou chears the heart o' drooping Care;
Thou strings the nerves o' Labor-sair,
   At's weary toil;
Thou even brightens dark Despair,
   Wi' gloomy smile.

Aft, clad in massy, siller weed,
Wi' Gentles thou erects thy head;
Yet humbly kind, in time o' need,
   The *poor man's* wine;
His wee drap pirratch or his bread,
   Thou kitchens fine.

Thou art the life o' public haunts;
But thee, what were our fairs and rants?
Ev'n godly meetings o' the saunts,
   By thee inspir'd,
When gaping they besiege the *tents*,
   Are doubly fir'd.

That *merry night* we get the corn in,
O sweetly, then, thou reams the horn in!
Or reekan on a *New-year-mornin*
                    In cog or bicker,
An' just a wee drap *sp'ritual burn* in,
                    An' gusty sucker!

When Vulcan gies his bellys breath,
An' Ploughmen gather wi' their graith,
O rare! to see thee fizz an' freath
                    I' the lugget caup!
Then *Burnewin* comes on like death
                    At ev'ry chap.

Nae mercy, then, for airn or steel;
The brawnie, banie, ploughman-chiel
Brings hard owrehip, wi' sturdy wheel,
                    The strong forehammer,
Till block an' studdie ring an' reel
                    Wi' dinsome clamour.

When skirling weanies see the light,
Thou maks the gossips clatter bright,
How fumbling coofs their dearies slight,
                    Wae worth them for't!
While healths gae round to him wha, *tight*,
                    Gies famous sport.

When neebors anger at a plea,
An' just as wud as wud can be,
How easy can the *barley-brie*
                    Cement the quarrel!
It's aye the cheapest lawyer's fee
                    To taste the barrel.

Alake! that e'er my *Muse* has reason,
To wyte her countrymen wi' treason!
But monie daily weet their weason
                    Wi' liquors nice,
An' hardly, in a winter season,
                    E'er spier her price.

Wae worth that *Brandy*, burnan trash!
Fell source o' monie a pain an' brash!
Twins monie a poor, doylt, druken hash
                    O' half his days;
An' sends, beside, auld *Scotland's* cash
                    To her warst faes.

Ye Scots wha wish auld Scotland well,
Ye chief, to you my tale I tell,
Poor, plackless devils like *mysel*,
                    It sets you ill,
Wi' bitter, dearthfu' *wines* to mell,
                    Or foreign gill.

May *gravels* round his blather wrench,
An' *gouts* torment him, inch by inch,
Wha twists his gruntle wi' a glunch
                    O' sour disdain,
Out owre a glass o' *Whisky-punch*
                    Wi' honest men!

O *Whisky*! soul o' plays an' pranks!
Accept a *Bardie's* gratefu' thanks!
When wanting thee, what tuneless cranks
                    Are my poor verses!
Thou comes – they rattle i' their ranks
                    At ither's arses!

Thee, *Ferintosh*! O sadly lost!
Scotland lament frae coast to coast!
Now colic-grips, an' barkin hoast,
                    May kill us a';
For loyal Forbes' *charter'd boast*
                    Is ta'en awa!

Thae curst horse-leeches o' th' Excise,
Wha mak the *Whisky stells* their prize!
Haud up thy han' *Deil*! ance, twice, *thrice*!
                    There, sieze the blinkers!
An' bake them up in brunstane pies
                    For poor damn'd *Drinkers*.

Fortune, if thou'll but gie me still
Hale breeks, a scone, an' *whisky gill*,
An' rowth o' *rhyme* to rave at will,
                    Tak a' the rest,
An' deal't about as thy blind skill
                    Directs thee best.

Address to the Deil

O Prince, O chief of many throned pow'rs,
That led th' embattl'd Seraphim to war –
                              Milton

O Thou, whatever title suit thee!
Auld Hornie, Satan, Nick, or Clootie!
Wha in yon cavern grim an' sootie,
                    Clos'd under hatches,
Spairges about the brunstane cootie,
                    To scaud poor wretches!

Hear me, *auld Hangie*, for a wee,
An' let poor, *damned bodies* bee;
I'm sure sma' pleasure it can gie,
                    Ev'n to a *deil*,
To skelp an' scaud poor dogs like me,
                    An' hear us squeel!

Great is thy pow'r, an' great thy fame;
Far kend an' noted is thy name;
An' tho' yon *lowan heugh's* thy hame,
                    Thou travels far;
An' faith! thou's neither lag nor lame,
                    Nor blate nor scaur.

Whyles, ranging like a roaran lion,
For prey, a' holes an' corners tryin;
Whyles, on the strong-wing'd tempest flyin,
                    Tirlan the *kirks*;
Whyles, in the human bosom pryin,
                    Unseen thou lurks.

I've heard my rev'rend *Graunie* say,
In lanely glens ye like to stray;
Or where auld, ruin'd castles, gray,
                    Nod to the moon,
Ye fright the nightly wand'rer's way,
                    Wi' eldritch croon.

When twilight did my *Graunie* summon,
To say her prayers, douse, honest woman!
Aft 'yont the dyke she's heard you bumman,
                    Wi' eerie drone;
Or, rustling, thro' the boortries coman,
                    Wi' heavy groan.

Ae dreary, windy, winter night,
The stars shot down wi' sklentan light,
Wi' you, *myself*, I gat a fright,
                    Ayont the lough;
Ye, like a *rass-buss*, stood in sight,
                    Wi' waving sugh.

The cudgel in my nieve did shake,
Each bristl'd hair stood like a stake,
When wi' an eldritch, stoor *quaick, quaick*,
                    Amang the springs,
Awa ye squatter'd like a *drake*,
                    On whistling wings.

Let *Warlocks* grim, an' wither'd *Hags*,
Tell how wi' you on ragweed nags,
They skim the muirs an' dizzy crags,
                    Wi' wicked speed;
And in kirk-yards renew their leagues,
                    Owre howcket dead.

Thence, countra wives, wi' toil an' pain,
May plunge an' plunge the *kirn* in vain;
For Oh! the yellow treasure's taen
        By witching skill;
An' dawtet, twal-pint *Hawkie's* gane
        As yell's the bill.

Thence, mystic knots mak great abuse,
On *Young-Guidmen*, fond, keen an' croose;
When the best *wark-lume* i' the house,
        By cantraip wit,
Is instant made no worth a louse,
        Just at the bit.

When thowes dissolve the snawy hoord,
An' float the jinglan icy boord,
Then *water-kelpies* haunt the foord,
        By your direction,
An' nighted trav'llers are allur'd
        To their destruction.

An' aft your moss-traversing *spunkies*
Decoy the wight that late an' drunk is:
The bleezan, curst, mischievous monkies
        Delude his eyes,
Till in some miry slough he sunk is,
        Ne'er mair to rise.

When Mason's mystic *word* an' *grip*,
In storms an' tempests raise you up,
Some cock or cat, your rage maun stop,
        Or, strange to tell!
The *youngest brother* ye wad whip
        Aff straught to Hell.

Lang syne in Eden's bonie yard,
When youthfu' lovers first were pair'd,
An' all the Soul of Love they shar'd,
          The raptur'd hour,
Sweet on the fragrant, flow'ry swaird,
          In shady bow'r.

Then you, ye auld, snick-drawing dog!
Ye cam to Paradise incog,
An' play'd on man a cursed brogue,
          (Black be your fa'!)
An' gied the infant warld a shog,
          'Maist ruin'd a'.

D'ye mind that day, when in a bizz,
Wi' reeket duds, an' reestet gizz,
Ye did present your smoutie phiz,
          'Mang better folk,
An' sklented on the *man of Uzz*,
          Your spitefu' joke?

An how ye gat him i' your thrall,
An' brak him out o' house an' hal',
While scabs an' botches did him gall,
          Wi' bitter claw,
An' lows'd his ill-tongu'd, wicked *scrawl*
          Was warst ava?

But a' your doings to rehearse,
Your wily snares an' fechtin fierce,
Sin' that day *Michael did you pierce,
          Down to this time,
Wad ding a *Lallan* tongue, or *Erse*,
          In Prose or Rhyme.

* Vide Milton, [*Paradise Lost*] Book 6th. [RB]

An' now, auld *Cloots*, I ken ye're thinkan,
A certain *Bardie's* rantin, drinkin,
Some luckless hour will send him linkan,
                    To your black pit;
But faith! he'll turn a corner jinkan,
                    An' cheat you yet.

But fare-you-weel, auld *Nickie-ben*!
O wad ye tak a thought an' men'!
Ye aiblens might – I dinna ken –
                    Still hae a *stake* –
I'm wae to think upo' yon den,
                    Ev'n for your sake!

Extempore to Gavin Hamilton.
Stanzas on Naething

To you, Sir, this summons I've sent,
    Pray, whip till the pownie is fraething;
But if you demand what I want,
    I honestly answer you – naething. –

Ne'er scorn a poor Poet like me,
    For idly just living and breathing,
While people of every degree
    Are busy employed about – naething. –

Poor Centum per centum may fast,
    And grumble his hurdies their claithing;
He'll find, when the balance is cast,
    He's gane to the devil for – naething. –

The Courtier cringes and bows,
    Ambition has likewise its plaything;
A Coronet beams on his brows,
    And what is a Coronet? – naething. –

Some quarrel the Presbyter gown,
    Some quarrel Episcopal graithing,
But every good fellow will own
    Their quarrel is all about – naething. –

The lover may sparkle and glow,
    Approaching his bonie bit gay thing;
But marriage will soon let him know,
    He's gotten a buskit up naething. –

The Poet may jingle and rhyme,
In hopes of a laureate wreathing,
And when he has wasted his time,
He's kindly rewarded with naething. –

The thundering bully may rage,
And swagger and swear like a heathen;
But collar him fast, I'll engage
You'll find that his courage is naething. –

Last night with a feminine Whig,
A Poet she could na put faith in,
But soon we grew lovingly big,
I taught her, her terrors were naething. –

Her Whigship was wonderful pleased,
But charmingly tickled wi' ae thing;
Her fingers I lovingly squeezed,
And kiss'd her and promised her – naething. –

The priest anathemas may threat,
Predicament, Sir, that we're baith in;
But when honor's reveille is beat,
The holy artillery's naething. –

And now I must mount on the wave,
My voyage perhaps there is death in;
But what of a watery grave!
The drowning a Poet is naething. –

And now as grim death's in my thought,
To you, Sir, I make this bequeathing:
My service as long as ye've ought,
And my friendship, by God, when ye've naething. –

To a Mountain Daisy
On Turning One Down with the Plough in April – 1786

Wee, modest, crimson-tipped flow'r,
Thou's met me in an evil hour;
For I maun crush amang the stoure
         Thy slender stem:
To spare thee now is past my pow'r,
           Thou bonie gem.

Alas! it's no thy neebor sweet,
The bonie *lark*, companion meet!
Bending thee 'mang the dewy weet!
         Wi' speckl'd breast,
When upward-springing, blythe, to greet
           The purpling East.

Cauld blew the bitter-biting *North*
Upon thy early, humble birth;
Yet chearfully thou glinted forth
         Amid the storm,
Scarce rear'd above the *Parent-earth*
           Thy tender form.

The flaunting *flow'rs* our gardens yield,
High-shelt'ring woods and wa's maun shield,
But thou, beneath the random bield
         O' clod or stane,
Adorns the histie *stibble-field*,
           Unseen, alane.

There, in thy scanty mantle clad,
Thy snawy bosom sun-ward spread,
Thou lifts thy unassuming head
        In humble guise;
But now the *share* uptears thy bed,
        And low thou lies!

Such is the fate of artless Maid,
Sweet *flow'ret* of the rural shade!
By love's simplicity betray'd,
        And guileless trust,
Till she, like thee, all soil'd, is laid
        Low i' the dust.

Such is the fate of simple Bard,
On life's rough ocean luckless starr'd!
Unskilful he to note the card
        Of *prudent lore*,
Till billows rage, and gales blow hard,
        And whelm him o'er!

Such fate to *suff'ring worth* is giv'n,
Who long with wants and woes has striv'n,
By human pride or cunning driv'n
        To mis'ry's brink,
Till wrench'd of every stay but Heav'n,
        He, ruin'd, sink!

Ev'n thou who mourn'st the *Daisy's* fate;
That fate is thine – no distant date;
Stern Ruin's *plough-share* drives, elate,
        Full on thy bloom,
Till crush'd beneath the *furrow's* weight,
        Shall be thy doom!

Epistle to a Young Friend
May – 1786

I lang hae thought, my youthfu' friend,
  A something to have sent you,
Though it should serve nae other end
  Than just a kind memento;
But how the subject theme may gang,
  Let time and chance determine;
Perhaps it may turn out a sang;
  Perhaps turn out a sermon.

Ye'll try the world soon my lad,
  And Andrew dear believe me,
Ye'll find mankind an unco squad,
  And muckle they may grieve ye:
For care and trouble set your thought,
  Ev'n when your end's attained;
And a' your views may come to nought,
  Where ev'ry nerve is strain'd.

I'll no say, men are villains a';
  The real, harden'd wicked,
Wha hae nae check but *human law*,
  Are to a few restricked:
But Och, mankind are unco weak,
  An' little to be trusted;
If *Self* the wavering balance shake,
  It's rarely right adjusted!

Yet they wha fa' in Fortune's strife,
    Their fate we should na censure,
For still th' *important end* of life,
    They equally may answer:
A man may hae an *honest heart*,
    Tho' poortith hourly stare him;
A man may tak a neebor's part,
    Yet hae nae *cash* to spare him.

Ay free, aff han', your story tell,
    When wi' a bosom crony;
But still keep something to yoursel
    Ye scarcely tell to ony.
Conceal yoursel as weel's you can
    Frae critical dissection;
But keek thro' ev'ry other man,
    Wi' sharpen'd, sly inspection.

The *sacred lowe* o' weel plac'd love,
    Luxuriantly indulge it;
But never tempt th' *illicit rove*,
    Tho' naething should divulge it:
I wave the quantum o' the sin;
    The hazard of concealing;
But Och! it hardens *a' within*,
    And petrifies the feeling!

To catch Dame Fortune's golden smile,
    Assiduous wait upon her;
And gather gear by ev'ry wile,
    That's justify'd by Honor:
Not for to *hide* it in a *hedge*,
    Nor for a *train-attendant*;
But for the glorious priviledge
    Of being *independant*.

The *fear o' Hell's* a hangman's whip,
  To haud the wretch in order;
But where ye feel your *Honor* grip,
  Let that ay be your border:
Its slightest touches, instant pause –
  Debar a' side-pretences;
And resolutely keep its laws,
  Uncaring consequences.

The great Creator to revere,
  Must sure become the *Creature*;
But still the preaching cant forbear,
  And ev'n the rigid feature:
Yet ne'er with Wits prophane to range,
  Be complaisance extended;
An *atheist-laugh's* a poor exchange
  For *Deity offended*!

When ranting round in Pleasure's ring,
  Religion may be blinded;
Or if she give a *random-fling*,
  It may be little minded;
But when on Life we're tempest-driven,
  A Conscience but a canker –
A correspondence fix'd wi' Heav'n,
  Is sure a noble *anchor*!

Adieu, dear, amiable Youth!
  Your *heart* can ne'er be wanting!
May Prudence, Fortitude and Truth
  Erect your brow undaunting!
In *ploughman phrase* 'God send you speed,'
  Still daily to grow wiser;
And may ye better reck the *rede*,
  Than ever did th' *Adviser*!

Lines Written on a Bank-Note

Wae worth thy pow'r, thou cursed leaf!
Fell source of a' my woe and grief!
For lake o' thee I've lost my lass;
For lake o' thee I scrimp my glass;
I see the children of Affliction
Unaided, thro' thy curs'd restriction.
I've seen the Oppressor's cruel smile
Amid his hapless victim's spoil;
And for thy potence vainly wish'd
To crush the villain in the dust:
For lake o' thee I leave this much-loved shore,
Never perhaps to greet Old Scotland more!

R. B.
Kyle

Address of Beelzebub

To the Right Honorable the Earl of Breadalbane, President of the Right Honorable the Highland Society, which met on the 23rd of May last, at the Shakespeare, Covent Garden, *to concert ways and means to frustrate the designs of five hundred Highlanders who, as the Society were informed by Mr M'Kenzie of Applecross, were so audacious as to attempt an escape from their lawful lords and masters whose property they are, by emigrating from the lands of Mr Macdonald of Glengary to the wilds of Canada, in search of that fantastic thing – Liberty –*

Long life, my lord, an' health be yours,
Unskaith'd by hunger'd Highland boors!
Lord grant nae duddie, desperate beggar,
Wi' dirk, claymore, or rusty trigger,
May twin auld Scotland o' a life
She likes – as Butchers like a knife!

Faith, you and Applecross were right
To keep the Highlan' hounds in sight!
I doubt na! they wad bid nae better
Than let them ance out owre the water;
Then up amang thae lakes an' seas,
They'll mak what rules and laws they please:
Some daring Hancocke, or a Frankline,
May set their Highlan' bluid a-ranklin;
Some Washington again may head them,
Or some Montgomery, fearless, lead them;
Till God knows what may be effected,
When by such heads and hearts directed.

Poor, dunghill sons of dirt an' mire,
May to Patrician rights aspire;
Nae sage North now, nor sager Sackville,
To watch an' premier owre the pack vile!
An' whare will ye get Howes an' Clintons
To bring them to a right repentance,
To cowe the rebel generation,
An' save the honor o' the nation?
They, an' be damned! what right hae they
To meat or sleep or light o' day,
Far less to riches, pow'r or freedom,
But what your lordships please to gie them?

But hear, my lord! Glengary, hear!
Your hand's owre light on them, I fear:
Your factors, greives, trustees and bailies,
I canna say but they do gaylies:
They lay aside a' tender mercies,
An' tirl the hallions to the birsies;
Yet while they're only poin'd and herriet,
They'll keep their stubborn Highlan spirit.
But smash them! crush them a' to spails!
And rot the dyvors i' the jails!
The young dogs, swinge them to the labour,
Let wark an' hunger mak them sober!
The hizzies, if they're oughtlins fausont,
Let them in Drury Lane be lesson'd!
An' if the wives, an' dirty brats,
Come thiggin at your doors an' yetts,
Flaffan wi' duds, an' grey wi' beese,
Frightan awa your deucks an' geese,
Get out a horsewhip, or a jowler,
The langest thong, the fiercest growler,

And gar the tatter'd gipseys pack
Wi' a' their bastarts on their back!

Go on, my lord! I lang to meet you,
An' in my 'house at hame' to greet you;
Wi' common lords ye shanna mingle:
The benmost newk, beside the ingle
At my right hand, assign'd your seat
'Tween Herod's hip, an' Polycrate,
Or (if you on your station tarrow)
Between Almagro and Pizarro;
A seat, I'm sure ye're weel deservin't;
An' till ye come – your humble servant,
                                        Beelzebub.

Hell,
1st June, Anno Mundi 5790

A Bard's Epitaph

Is there a whim-inspir'd fool,
Owre fast for thought, owre hot for rule,
Owre blate to seek, owre proud to snool,
        Let him draw near;
And o'er this grassy heap sing dool,
        And drap a tear.

Is there a Bard of rustic song,
Who, noteless, steals the crouds among,
That weekly this area throng,
        O, pass not by!
But with a frater-feeling strong,
        Here, heave a sigh.

Is there a man whose judgment clear,
Can others teach the course to steer,
Yet runs, himself, life's mad career,
        Wild as the wave,
Here pause – and thro' the starting tear,
        Survey this grave.

The poor Inhabitant below
Was quick to learn and wise to know,
And keenly felt the friendly glow,
        And *softer flame*;
But thoughtless follies laid him low,
        And stain'd his name!

Reader attend – whether thy soul
Soars fancy's flights beyond the pole,
Or darkling grubs this earthly hole,
        In low pursuit,
Know, prudent, cautious, *self-controul*
        Is Wisdom's root.

To a Haggis

Fair fa' your honest, sonsie face,
Great Chieftan o' the Puddin-race!
Aboon them a' ye tak your place,
              Painch, tripe, or thairm:
Weel are ye wordy of a *grace*
              As lang's my arm.

The groaning trencher there ye fill,
Your hurdies like a distant hill,
Your *pin* wad help to mend a mill
              In time o' need,
While thro' your pores the dews distil
              Like amber bead.

His knife see Rustic-labour dight,
An' cut you up wi' ready slight,
Trenching your gushing entrails bright
              Like onie ditch;
And then, O what a glorious sight,
              Warm-reekin, rich!

Then, horn for horn they stretch an' strive,
Deil tak the hindmost, on they drive,
Till a' their weel-swall'd kytes belyve
              Are bent like drums;
Then auld Guidman, maist like to rive,
              Bethankit hums.

Is there that owre his French *ragout*,
Or *olio* that wad staw a sow,
Or *fricassee* wad mak her spew
            Wi' perfect sconner,
Looks down wi' sneering, scornfu' view
            On sic a dinner?

Poor devil! see him owre his trash,
As feckless as a wither'd rash,
His spindle-shank a guid whip-lash,
            His nieve a nit;
Thro' bluidy flood or field to dash,
            O how unfit!

But mark the Rustic, *haggis-fed*,
The trembling earth resounds his tread,
Clap in his walie nieve a blade,
            He'll mak it whissle;
An' legs, an' arms, an' heads will sned,
            Like taps o' thrissle.

Ye Pow'rs wha mak mankind your care,
An' dish them out their bill o' fare,
Auld Scotland wants nae skinking ware
            That jaups in luggies;
But, if ye wish her gratefu' pray'r,
            Gie her a *Haggis*!

My Peggy's Face

My Peggy's face, my Peggy's form,
The frost of hermit age might warm;
My Peggy's worth, my Peggy's mind,
Might charm the first of humankind.
I love my Peggy's angel air,
Her face so truly heavn'ly fair,
Her native grace so void of art,
But I adore my Peggy's heart.

The lily's hue, the rose's die,
The kindling lustre of an eye;
Who but owns their magic sway,
Who but knows they will decay!
The tender thrill, the pitying tear,
The gen'rous purpose nobly dear,
The gentle look that Rage disarms,
These are all Immortal charms.

O'er the Water to Charlie
(TUNE: SHAWNBOY)

Come boat me o'er, come row me o'er,
Come boat me o'er to Charlie;
I'll gie John Ross another bawbee,
To boat me o'er to Charlie.

    We'll o'er the water, we'll o'er the sea,
    We'll o'er the water to Charlie;
    Come weal, come woe, we'll gather and go,
    And live or die wi' Charlie.

I lo'e weel my Charlie's name,
Tho' some there be abhor him:
But O, to see auld Nick gaun hame,
And Charlie's faes before him!
    We'll o'er &c.

I swear and vow by moon and stars,
And sun that shines so early!
If I had twenty thousand lives,
I'd die as aft for Charlie.
    We'll o'er &c.

Rattlin, Roarin Willie

O rattlin, roarin Willie,
  O he held to the fair,
An' for to sell his fiddle
  And buy some other ware;
But parting wi' his fiddle,
  The saut tear blin't his e'e;
And rattlin, roarin Willie
  Ye're welcome hame to me.

O Willie, come sell your fiddle,
  O sell your fiddle sae fine;
O Willie, come sell your fiddle,
  And buy a pint o' wine;
If I should sell my fiddle,
  The warl would think I was mad,
For mony a rantin day
  My fiddle and I hae had.

As I cam by Crochallan
  I cannily keekit ben,
Rattlin, roarin Willie
  Was sitting at yon boord-en',
Sitting at yon boord-en',
  And amang guid companie:
Rattlin, roarin Willie,
  You're welcome hame to me.

On a Schoolmaster

Here lie Willie Michie's banes;
O, Satan! When ye tak him,
Gie him the schoolin' o' your weans,
For clever de'ils he'll mak 'em!

Tam Glen
(TUNE: MERRY BEGGARS)

My heart is a breaking, dear Tittie,
   Some counsel unto me come len',
To anger them a' is a pity,
   But what will I do wi' Tam Glen?

I'm thinking, wi' sic a braw fellow,
   In poortith I might mak a fen':
What care I in riches to wallow,
   If I mauna marry Tam Glen.

There's Lowrie the laird o' Dumeller,
   'Gude day to you brute' he comes ben:
He brags and he blaws o' his siller,
   But when will he dance like Tam Glen.

My Minnie does constantly deave me,
   And bids me beware o' young men;
They flatter, she says, to deceive me,
   But wha can think sae o' Tam Glen.

My Daddie says, gin I'll forsake him,
   He'll gie me gude hunder marks ten:
But if it's ordain'd I maun take him,
   O wha will I get but Tam Glen?

Yestreen at the Valentines' dealing,
   My heart to my mou gied a sten;
For thrice I drew ane without failing,
   And thrice it was written, Tam Glen.

The last Halloween I was waukin
   My droukit sark-sleeve, as ye ken;
His likeness cam up the house staukin,
   And the very grey breeks o' Tam Glen!

Come counsel, dear Tittie, don't tarry;
   I'll gie you my bonie black hen,
Gif ye will advise me to marry
   The lad I lo'e dearly, Tam Glen.

Auld Lang Syne
(TUNE: FOR OLD LONG SINE MY JO)

Should auld acquaintance be forgot
    And never brought to mind?
Should auld acquaintance be forgot,
    And auld lang syne!

    For auld lang syne my jo,
        For auld lang syne,
    We'll tak a *cup o' kindness yet,
        For auld lang syne.

And surely ye'll be your pint stowp!
    And surely I'll be mine!
And we'll tak a cup o' kindness yet,
    For auld lang syne.
        For auld &c.

We twa hae run about the braes,
    And pou'd the gowans fine;
But we've wander'd mony a weary fitt,
    Sin auld lang syne.
        For auld &c.

We twa hae paidl'd in the burn,
    Frae morning sun till dine;
But seas between us braid hae roar'd,
    Sin auld lang syne.
        For auld &c.

* Some Sing, Kiss in place of Cup. [RB]

And there's a hand, my trusty fiere!
   And gie's a hand o' thine!
And we'll tak a right gude-willie-waught,
   For auld lang syne.
      For auld &c.

Elegy on the Year 1788

For Lords or kings I dinna mourn,
E'en let them die – for that they're born!
But oh! prodigious to reflect,
A *Towmont*, Sirs, is gane to wreck!
O *Eighty-eight*, in thy sma' space
What dire events ha'e taken place!
Of what enjoyments thou hast reft us!
In what a pickle thou has left us!

The Spanish empire's tint a head,
An' my auld teethless Bawtie's dead;
The toolzie's teugh 'tween Pitt an' Fox,
An' our guidwife's wee birdy cocks;
The tane is game, a bluidy devil,
But to the *hen-birds* unco civil;
The tither's dour, has nae sic breedin',
But better stuff ne'er claw'd a midden!

Ye ministers, come mount the pulpit,
An' cry till ye be haerse an' rupit;
For *Eighty-eight* he wish'd you weel,
An' gied you a' baith gear an' meal;
E'en mony a plack, an' mony a peck,
Ye ken yoursels, for little feck!

Ye bonny lasses, dight your een,
For some o' you ha'e tint a frien';
In *Eighty-eight*, ye ken, was ta'en
What ye'll ne'er ha'e to gi'e again.

Observe the very nowt an' sheep,
How dowff an' dowie now they creep;
Nay, even the yirth itsel' does cry,
For Embro' wells are grutten dry.

O *Eighty-nine*, thou's but a bairn,
An' no owre auld, I hope, to learn!
Thou beardless boy, I pray tak' care,
Thou now has got thy Daddy's chair,
Nae hand-cuff'd, mizl'd, haff-shackl'd *Regent*,
But, like himsel', a full free agent.
Be sure ye follow out the plan
Nae war than he did, honest man!
As muckle better as you can.

January 1, 1789

Afton Water

Flow gently, sweet Afton, among thy green braes,
Flow gently, I'll sing thee a song in thy praise;
My Mary's asleep by thy murmuring stream,
Flow gently, sweet Afton, disturb not her dream.

Thou stock dove whose echo resounds thro' the glen,
Ye wild whistling blackbirds in yon thorny den,
Thou green crested lapwing thy screaming forbear,
I charge you disturb not my slumbering Fair.

How lofty, sweet Afton, thy neighbouring hills,
Far mark'd with the courses of clear, winding rills;
There daily I wander as noon rises high,
My flocks and my Mary's sweet cot in my eye.

How pleasant thy banks and green vallies below,
Where wild in the woodlands the primroses blow;
There oft as mild ev'ning weeps over the lea,
The sweet scented birk shades my Mary and me.

Thy chrystal stream, Afton, how lovely it glides,
And winds by the cot where my Mary resides;
How wanton thy waters her snowy feet lave,
As gath'ring sweet flow'rets she stems thy clear wave.

Flow gently, sweet Afton, among thy green braes,
Flow gently, sweet river, the theme of my lays;
My Mary's asleep by thy murmuring stream,
Flow gently, sweet Afton, disturb not her dream.

To a Gentleman Who Had Sent Him a Newspaper and Offered to Continue It Free of Expense

Kind Sir, I've read your paper through,
And faith, to me, 'twas really new!
How guessed ye, Sir, what maist I wanted?
This mony a day I've grain'd and gaunted,
To ken what French mischief was brewin;
Or what the drumlie Dutch were doin;
That vile doup-skelper, Emperor Joseph,
If Venus yet had got his nose off;
Or how the collieshangie works
Atween the Russians and the Turks;
Or if the Swede, before he halt,
Would play anither Charles the twalt:
If Denmark, any body spak o't;
Or Poland, wha had now the tack o't;
How cut-throat Prussian blades were hingin;
How libbet Italy was singin;
If Spaniard, Portuguese or Swiss,
Were sayin or takin aught amiss:
Or how our merry lads at hame,
In Britain's court kept up the game:
How royal George, the Lord leuk o'er him!
Was managing St Stephen's quorum;
If sleekit Chatham Will was livin,
Or glaikit Charlie got his nieve in;
How daddie Burke the plea was cookin,
If Warren Hasting's neck was yeukin;
How cesses, stents, and fees were rax'd,
Or if bare arses yet were tax'd;

The news o' princes, dukes and earls,
Pimps, sharpers, bawds, and opera-girls;
If that daft buckie, Geordie Wales,
Was threshin still at hizzies' tails,
Or if he was grown oughtlins douser,
And no a perfect kintra cooser,
A' this and mair I never heard of;
And but for you I might despair'd of.
So gratefu', back your news I send you,
And pray, a' gude things may attend you!

Ellisland, Monday-morning, 1790

Lassie Lie Near Me
(TUNE: LADDIE LIE NEAR ME)

Lang hae we parted been,
Lassie my dearie;
Now we are met again,
Lassie lie near me.

    Near me, near me,
    Lassie lie near me
    Lang hast thou lien thy lane,
    Lassie lie near me.

A' that I hae endur'd,
Lassie, my dearie,
Here in thy arms is cur'd,
Lassie lie near me.
    Near me, &c.

My Love She's But a Lassie Yet

My love she's but a lassie yet,
My love she's but a lassie yet,
We'll let her stand a year or twa,
      She'll no be half sae saucy yet.

I rue the day I sought her O,
I rue the day I sought her O,
Wha gets her needs na say he's woo'd,
      But he may say he's bought her O.

Come draw a drap o' the best o't yet,
Come draw a drap o' the best o't yet:
Gae seek for pleasure where ye will,
      But here I never misst it yet.

We're a' dry wi' drinkin o't,
We're a' dry wi' drinkin o't:
The minister kisst the fidler's wife,
      He could na preach for thinkin o't.

Farewell to the Highlands
(TUNE: FAILTE NA MIOSG – THE MUSKET SALUTE)

My heart's in the Highlands, my heart is not here;
My heart's in the Highlands a chasing the deer;
A chasing the wild deer, and following the roe,
My heart's in the Highlands, wherever I go.
Farewell to the Highlands, farewell to the north,
The birth place of Valour, the country of Worth,
Wherever I wander, wherever I rove,
The hills of the Highlands for ever I love.

Farewell to the mountains high cover'd with snow;
Farewell to the straths and green vallies below:
Farewell to the forests and wild hanging woods;
Farewell to the torrents and loud pouring floods.
My heart's in the Highlands, my heart is not here,
My heart's in the Highlands, a chasing the deer:
Chasing the wild deer, and following the roe,
My heart's in the Highlands, wherever I go.

John Anderson My Jo

John Anderson my jo, John,
When we were first acquent;
Your locks were like the raven,
Your bony brow was brent;
But now your brow is beld, John,
Your locks are like the snaw;
But blessings on your frosty pow,
John Anderson my jo.

John Anderson my jo, John,
We clamb the hill the gither;
And mony a canty day, John,
We've had wi' ane anither:
Now we maun totter down, John,
And hand in hand we'll go:
And sleep the gither at the foot,
John Anderson my jo.

Tam o' Shanter. A Tale

Of Brownyis and of Bogillis full is this buke.
Gawin Douglas

When chapman billies leave the street,
And drouthy neebors, neebors meet,
As market-days are wearing late,
An' folk begin to tak the gate;
While we sit bousing at the nappy,
An' getting fou and unco happy,
We think na on the lang Scots miles,
The mosses, waters, slaps and styles,
That lie between us and our hame,
Whare sits our sulky sullen dame,
Gathering her brows like gathering storm,
Nursing her wrath to keep it warm.

This truth fand honest *Tam o' Shanter*,
As he frae Ayr ae night did canter,
(Auld Ayr wham ne'er a town surpasses,
For honest men and bonny lasses.)

O *Tam*! hadst thou but been sae wise,
As ta'en thy ain wife *Kate's* advice!
She tauld thee weel thou was a skellum,
A blethering, blustering, drunken blellum;
That frae November till October,
Ae market day thou was nae sober;
That ilka melder, wi' the miller,
Thou sat as lang as thou had siller;

That ev'ry naig was ca'd a shoe on,
The smith and thee gat roaring fou on;
That at the Lord's house, ev'n on Sunday,
Thou drank wi' Kirkton Jean till Monday.
She prophesy'd that late or soon,
Thou would be found deep drown'd in Doon;
Or catch'd wi' warlocks in the mirk,
By *Alloway's* auld haunted kirk.

Ah, gentle dames! it gars me greet,
To think how mony counsels sweet,
How mony lengthen'd, sage advices,
The husband frae the wife despises!

But to our tale: Ae market night,
Tam had got planted unco right;
Fast by an ingle, bleezing finely,
Wi' reaming swats, that drank divinely;
And at his elbow, Souter *Johnny*,
His ancient, trusty, drouthy crony;
Tam lo'ed him like a vera brither;
They had been fou for weeks thegither.
The night drave on wi' sangs and clatter;
And ay the ale was growing better:
The landlady and *Tam* grew gracious,
Wi' favours, secret, sweet, and precious:
The Souter tauld his queerest stories;
The landlord's laugh was ready chorus:
The storm without might rair and rustle,
Tam did na mind the storm a whistle.

Care, mad to see a man sae happy,
E'en drown'd himself amang the nappy,

As bees flee hame wi' lades o' treasure,
The minutes wing'd their way wi' pleasure:
Kings may be blest, but *Tam* was glorious,
O'er a' the ills o' life victorious!

But pleasures are like poppies spread,
You seize the flow'r, its bloom is shed:
Or like the snow falls in the river,
A moment white – then melts forever;
Or like the borealis race,
That flit ere you can point their place;
Or like the rainbow's lovely form
Evanishing amid the storm. –
Nae man can tether time nor tide;
The hour approaches Tam maun ride;
That hour, o' night's black arch the key-stane,
That dreary hour he mounts his beast in;
And sic a night he taks the road in,
As ne'er poor sinner was abroad in.

The wind blew as 'twad blawn its last;
The rattling show'rs rose on the blast;
The speedy gleams the darkness swallow'd;
Loud, deep, and lang, the thunder bellow'd:
That night, a child might understand,
The Deil had business on his hand.

Weel mounted on his gray mare, *Meg*,
A better never lifted leg,
Tam skelpit on thro' dub and mire,
Despising wind, and rain, and fire;
Whiles holding fast his gude blue bonnet;
Whiles crooning o'er some auld Scots sonnet;

Whiles glow'ring round wi' prudent cares,
Lest bogles catch him unawares:
Kirk-Alloway was drawing nigh,
Whare ghaists and houlets nightly cry. –

By this time he was cross the ford,
Where in the snaw, the chapman smoor'd;
And past the birks and meikle stane,
Whare drunken *Charlie* brak's neck-bane;
And thro' the whins, and by the cairn,
Whare hunters fand the murder'd bairn;
And near the thorn, aboon the well,
Whare *Mungo's* mither hang'd hersel. –
Before him *Doon* pours all his floods:
The doubling storm roars thro' the woods:
The lightnings flash from pole to pole;
Near and more near the thunders roll:
When, glimmering thro' the groaning trees,
Kirk Alloway seem'd in a bleeze;
Thro' ilka bore the beams were glancing;
And loud resounded mirth and dancing. –

Inspiring bold *John Barleycorn*!
What dangers thou canst make us scorn!
Wi' tipenny, we fear nae evil;
Wi' usquebae we'll face the devil! –
The swats sae ream'd in *Tammie's* noddle,
Fair play, he car'd na deils a boddle.
But *Maggie* stood right sair astonish'd,
Till, by the heel and hand admonish'd,
She ventur'd forward on the light;
And, vow! *Tam* saw an unco sight!
Warlocks and witches in a dance;
Nae cotillion brent new frae *France*,

But hornpipes, jigs, strathspeys, and reels,
Put life and mettle in their heels,
A winnock-bunker in the east,
There sat auld Nick, in shape o' beast;
A towzie tyke, black, grim, and large,
To gie them music was his charge:
He screw'd the pipes and gart them skirl,
Till roof and rafters a' did dirl. –
Coffins stood round, like open presses,
That shaw'd the dead in their last dresses;
And by some devilish cantraip slight
Each in its cauld hand held a light. –
By which heroic *Tam* was able
To note upon the haly table,
A murderer's banes in gibbet airns;
Twa span-lang, wee, unchristen'd bairns;
A thief, new-cutted frae a rape,
Wi' his last gasp his gab did gape;
Five tomahawks, wi' blude red-rusted;
Five scymitars, wi' murder crusted;
A garter, which a babe had strangled;
A knife, a father's throat had mangled,
Whom his ain son o' life bereft,
The grey hairs yet stack to the heft;
Wi' mair o' horrible an' awefu',
Which ev'n to name wad be unlawfu'.

    As *Tammie* glowr'd, amaz'd, and curious,
The mirth and fun grew fast and furious;
The piper loud and louder blew;
The dancers quick and quicker flew;
They reel'd, they set, they cross'd, they cleekit,
Till ilka carlin swat and reekit,

And coost her duddies to the wark,
And linket at it in her sark!

Now *Tam*, O *Tam*! had thae been queans,
A' plump and strapping in their teens,
Their sarks, instead o' creeshie flannen,
Been snaw-white seventeen hunder linnen!
Thir breeks o' mine, my only pair,
That ance were plush, o' gude blue hair,
I wad hae gi'en them off my hurdies,
For ae blink o' the bonie burdies!

But wither'd beldams, auld and droll,
Rigwoodie hags wad spean a foal,
Lowping and flinging on a crummock,
I wonder didna turn thy stomach.

But *Tam* kend what was what fu' brawlie,
There was ae winsome wench and wawlie,
That night enlisted in the core,
(Lang after kend on *Carrick* shore;
For mony a beast to dead she shot,
And perish'd mony a bony boat,
And shook baith meikle corn and bear,
And kept the countryside in fear)
Her cutty sark, o' Paisley harn,
That while a lassie she had worn,
In longitude tho' sorely scanty,
It was her best, and she was vauntie. –
Ah! little kend thy reverend grannie,
That sark she coft for her wee Nannie,
Wi' twa pund Scots ('twas a' her riches)
Wad ever grac'd a dance o' witches!

But here my Muse her wing maun cour;
Sic flights are far beyond her pow'r;
To sing how Nannie lap and flang,
(A souple jade she was, and strang),
And how *Tam* stood, like ane bewitch'd,
And thought his very een enrich'd;
Ev'n Satan glowr'd, and fidg'd fu' fain,
And hotch'd and blew wi' might and main:
Till first ae caper, syne anither,
Tam tint his reason a' thegither,
And roars out, 'Weel done, Cutty-sark!'
And in an instant all was dark:
And scarcely had he Maggie rallied,
When out the hellish legion sallied.

As bees bizz out wi' angry fyke,
When plundering herds assail their byke,
As open pussie's mortal foes,
When pop! she starts before their nose;
As eager runs the market-crowd,
When 'Catch the thief!' resounds aloud;
So Maggie runs, the witches follow,
Wi' mony an eldritch skreech and hollow.

Ah, *Tam*! Ah, *Tam*! thou'll get thy fairin!
In hell they'll roast thee like a herrin!
In vain thy *Kate* awaits thy comin!
Kate soon will be a woefu' woman!
Now, do thy speedy utmost, Meg,
And win the key-stane* of the brig;

---

* It is a well known fact that witches, or any evil spirits, have no power
to follow a poor wight any farther than the middle of the next running
stream. – It may be proper likewise to mention to the benighted traveller,
that when he falls in with *bogles*, whatever danger there may be in his
going forward, there is much more hazard in turning back. [RB]

There at them thou thy tail may toss,
A running stream they dare na cross.
But ere the key-stane she could make,
The fient a tale she had to shake!
For Nannie, far before the rest,
Hard upon noble Maggie prest,
And flew at Tam wi' furious ettle;
But little wist she Maggie's mettle –
Ae spring brought off her master hale,
But left behind her ain gray tail:
The carlin claught her by the rump,
And left poor Maggie scarce a stump.

Now, wha this tale o' truth shall read,
Ilk man and mother's son, take heed:
Whene'er to drink you are inclin'd,
Or cutty sarks run in your mind,
Think, ye may buy the joys o'er dear,
Remember Tam o' Shanter's mare.

The Banks o' Doon
(TUNE: CALEDONIAN HUNT'S DELIGHT)

Ye banks and braes o' bonie Doon,
　　How can ye bloom sae fresh and fair;
How can ye chant, ye little birds,
　　And I sae weary fu' o' care!
Thou'll break my heart, thou warbling bird,
　　That wantons thro' the flowering thorn:
Thou minds me o' departed joys,
　　Departed never to return.

Oft hae I rov'd by bonie Doon,
　　To see the rose and woodbine twine
And ilka bird sang o' its luve,
　　And fondly sae did I o' mine.
Wi' lightsome heart I pu'd a rose,
　　Fu' sweet upon its thorny tree;
And my fause luver staw my rose,
　　But ah! he left the thorn wi' me.

Ye Jacobites By Name

Ye Jacobites by name, give an ear, give an ear;
Ye Jacobites by name, give an ear;
Ye Jacobites by name,
Your fautes I will proclaim,
Your doctrines I maun blame –
You shall hear.

What is right and what is wrang, by the law, by the
    law?
What is right and what is wrang, by the law?
What is right and what is wrang?
A short sword and a lang,
A weak arm and a strang
For to draw.

What makes heroic strife, famed afar, famed afar?
What makes heroic strife, famed afar?
What makes heroic strife?
To whet th' assassin's knife,
Or hunt a parent's life
Wi' bluidie war.

Then let your schemes alone, in the State, in the State;
Then let your schemes alone in the State;
Then let your schemes alone,
Adore the rising sun,
And leave a man undone
To his fate.

Fareweel to a' Our Scottish Fame

Fareweel to a' our Scottish fame,
Fareweel our ancient glory!
Fareweel even to the Scottish name,
Sae fam'd in martial story!
Now Sark rins o'er the Solway sands,
And Tweed rins to the ocean,
To mark where England's province stands –
Such a parcel of rogues in a nation!

What force or guile could not subdue,
Thro' many warlike ages,
Is wrought now by a coward few,
For hireling traitors' wages.
The English steel we could disdain,
Secure in valour's station;
But English gold has been our bane –
Such a parcel of rogues in a nation!

O would, ere I had seen the day
That treason thus could sell us,
My auld grey head had lien in clay,
Wi' Bruce and loyal Wallace!
But pith and power, till my last hour,
I'll mak' this declaration;
We're bought and sold for English gold –
Such a parcel of rogues in a nation.

Ae Fond Kiss
(TUNE: RORY DALL'S PORT)

Ae fond kiss, and then we sever;
Ae farewell and then forever!
Deep in heart-wrung tears I'll pledge thee,
Warring sighs and groans I'll wage thee.

Who shall say that fortune grieves him
While the star of hope she leaves him?
Me, nae chearfu' twinkle lights me;
Dark despair around benights me.

I'll ne'er blame my partial fancy,
Naething could resist my Nancy:
But to see her, was to love her;
Love but her, and love for ever.

Had we never lov'd sae kindly,
Had we never lov'd sae blindly,
Never met – or never parted,
We had ne'er been broken-hearted.

Fare thee weel, thou first and fairest!
Fare thee weel, thou best and dearest!
Thine be ilka joy and treasure,
Peace, Enjoyment, Love and Pleasure!

Ae fond kiss, and then we sever;
Ae fareweel, Alas! for ever!
Deep in heart-wrung tears I'll pledge thee,
Warring sighs and groans I'll wage thee.

I Hae a Wife o' My Ain

I hae a wife o' my ain,
 I'll partake wi' naebody;
I'll tak Cuckold frae nane,
 I'll gie Cuckold to naebody.

I hae a penny to spend,
 There, thanks to naebody;
I hae naething to lend,
 I'll borrow frae naebody.

I am naebody's lord,
 I'll be slave to naebody;
I hae a gude braid sword,
 I'll tak dunts frae naebody.

I'll be merry and free,
 I'll be sad for naebody;
Naebody cares for me,
 I care for naebody.

Logan Water

O Logan, sweetly didst thou glide,
The day I was my Willie's bride;
And years sinsyne hae o'er us run,
Like Logan to the simmer sun.
But now thy flow'ry banks appear
Like drumlie winter, dark and drear,
While my dear lad maun face his faes,
Far, far frae me and Logan braes.

Again the merry month o' May
Has made our hills and vallies gay;
The birds rejoice in leafy bow'rs,
The bees hum round the breathing flow'rs:
Blythe morning lifts his rosy eye,
And ev'ning's tears are tears o' joy:
My soul, delightless, a' surveys,
While Willie's far frae Logan braes.

Within yon milk-white hawthorn bush,
Amang her nestlings sits the thrush;
Her faithfu' mate will share her toil,
Or wi' his song her cares beguile: –
But I, wi' my sweet nurslings here,
Nae mate to help, nae mate to cheer,
Pass widow'd nights, and joyless days,
While Willie's far frae Logan braes.

O wae upon you, men o' state,
That brethren rouse in deadly hate!
As ye make mony a fond heart mourn,
Sae may it on your heads return!
Ye mind na, mid your cruel joys,
The widow's tears, the orphan's cries!
But soon may peace bring happy days,
And Willie hame to Logan braes!

Scots Wha Hae
(TUNE: HEY, TUTTI TAITIE)

Scots, wha hae wi' Wallace bled,
Scots, wham Bruce has aften led,
Welcome to your gory bed
        Or to victorie!

Now's the day, and now's the hour:
See the front o' battle lour,
See approach proud Edward's power –
        Chains and slaverie!

Wha will be a traitor knave?
Wha can fill a coward's grave?
Wha sae base as be a slave? –
        Let him turn, and flee!

Wha for Scotland's king and law
Freedom's sword will strongly draw,
Freeman stand or freeman fa',
        Let him follow me!

By Oppression's woes and pains,
By your sons in servile chains,
We will drain our dearest veins
        But they shall be free!

Lay the proud usurpers low!
Tyrants fall in every foe!
Liberty's in every blow! –
        Let us do, or die!

A Red, Red Rose
(TUNE: MAJOR GRAHAM)

My luve is like a red, red rose,
    That's newly sprung in June:
My luve is like the melodie,
    That's sweetly play'd in tune.
As fair art thou, my bonie lass,
    So deep in luve am I,
And I will luve thee still, my dear,
    Till a' the seas gang dry.

        } [twice]

Till a' the seas gang dry, my dear,
    And the rocks melt wi' the sun!
And I will luve thee still, my dear,
    While the sands o' life shall run.
And fare-thee-weel, my only luve,
    And fare-thee-weel a while!
And I will come again, my luve,
    Tho' it were ten-thousand mile.

        } [twice]

Sae Flaxen Were Her Ringlets
(TUNE: OONAGH'S WATERFALL)

Sae flaxen were her ringlets,
    Her eyebrows of a darker hue,
Bewitchingly o'erarching
    Twa laughing een o' bonie blue;
Her smiling, sae wyling,
    Wad make a wretch forget his woe;
What pleasure, what treasure,
    Unto these rosy lips to grow:
Such was my Chloris' bonie face,
    When first her bonie face I saw;
And ay my Chloris' dearest charm,
    She says, she lo'es me best of a'.

Like harmony her motion;
    Her pretty ancle is a spy,
Betraying fair proportion,
    Wad make a saint forget the sky.
Sae warming, sae charming,
    Her fauteless form and gracefu' air;
Ilk feature – auld Nature
    Declar'd that she could do nae mair:
Hers are the willing chains o' love,
    By conquering Beauty's sovereign law;
And ay my Chloris' dearest charm,
    She says, she lo'es me best of a'.

Let others love the city,
  And gaudy shew at sunny noon;
Give me the lonely valley,
  The dewy eve, and rising moon.
Fair beaming, and streaming
  Her silver light the boughs among;
While falling, recalling,
  The amorous thrush concludes his sang;
There, dearest Chloris, wilt thou rove
  By wimpling burn and leafy shaw,
And hear my vows o' truth and love,
  And say, thou lo'es me best of a'.

Ode to Spring
(TUNE: THE TITHER MORN)

When maukin bucks, at early f—s,
    In dewy glens are seen, Sir;
And birds, on boughs, take off their m—s,
    Amang the leaves sae green, Sir;
Latona's sun looks liquorish on
    Dame Nature's grand impètus,
Till his p—go rise, then westward flies
    To r–ger Madame Thetis.

Yon wandering rill that marks the hill,
    And glances o'er the brae, Sir,
Slides by a bower where many a flower
    Sheds fragrance on the day, Sir;
There Damon lay with Sylvia gay,
    To love they thought no crime, Sir;
The wild-birds sang, the echoes rang,
    While Damon's a–se beat time, Sir.

First, wi' the thrush, his thrust and push
    Had compass large and long, Sir;
The blackbird next, his tuneful text,
    Was bolder, clear and strong, Sir:
The linnet's lay came then in play,
    And the lark that soar'd aboon, Sir;
Till Damon, fierce, mistim'd his a—,
    And f—'d quite out o' tune, Sir.

Is There for Honest Poverty
(TUNE: FOR A' THAT)

Is there for honest poverty
  That hings his head, an' a' that?
The coward slave, we pass him by –
  We dare be poor for a' that!
      For a' that, an a' that,
        Our toils obscure, an' a' that,
        The rank is but the guinea's stamp,
          The man's the gowd for a' that.

What tho' on hamely fare we dine,
  Wear hodden grey, an' a' that?
Gie fools their silks, and knaves their wine –
  A man's a man for a' that!
      For a' that, an' a' that,
        Their tinsel show, an' a' that,
        The honest man, tho' e'er sae poor,
          Is king o' men for a' that.

Ye see yon birkie ca'd a lord,
  Wha struts, and stares, an' a' that;
Tho' hundreds worship at his word,
  He's but a coof for a' that.
      For a' that, an' a' that,
        His ribband, star, an' a' that,
        The man o' independent mind,
          He looks an' laughs at a' that.

A prince can mak a belted knight,
    A marquis, duke, an' a' that,
But an honest man's aboon his might –
    Gude faith, he mauna fa' that!
        For a' that, an' a' that,
            Their dignities, an a' that,
            The pith o' sense an' pride o' worth
            Are higher rank than a' that.

Then let us pray that come it may –
    As come it will, for a' that –
That sense and worth, o'er a' the earth
    Shall bear the gree, an' a' that;
        For a' that, an' a' that,
            It's comin yet for a' that,
            That man to man the world o'er,
            Shall brothers be for a' that.

Kirkcudbright Grace

Some have meat and cannot eat,
　Some cannot eat that want it:
But we have meat and we can eat,
　Sae let the Lord be thankit.

Charlie He's My Darling

'Twas on a Monday morning,
    Right early in the year,
That Charlie cam to our town,
    The young Chevalier.
            An' Charlie he's my darling,
            My darling, my darling,
            Charlie he's my darling, the young Chevalier.

As he was walking up the street,
    The city for to view,
O there he spied a bonie lass
    The window looking thro'. – An' Charlie &c.

Sae light's he jimped up the stair,
    And tirled at the pin;
And wha sae ready as hersel,
    To let the laddie in. – An' Charlie &c.

He set his Jenny on his knee,
    All in his Highland dress;
For brawlie weel he ken'd the way
    To please a bonie lass. – An' Charlie &c.

It's up yon hethery mountain,
    And down yon scroggy glen,
We daur na gang a milking,
    For Charlie and his men. – An' Charlie &c.

Glossary

a': all
aboon: above
agley: aslant, wrong
aiblins: perhaps
ain: own
airn: iron
aith: oath
aits: oats
ane: one
asklent: askew, awry
auldfarran: sagacious, prudent
ava: at all, of all
awnie: bearded
ayont: beyond

baith: both
bane: bone
banie: big-boned, muscular
bear the gree: to win the victory
beese: vermin
ben: in
benmost: innermost
bicker: wooden dish
bien: prosperous, comfortable
big: to build
bill: bull
billie: fellow, comrade
birk: birch

birkie: clever fellow
birsies: bristles
bizz: bustle
blate: bashful
blather: bladder
bleezan: blazing
blellum: babbler, idle-talking fellow
bleth'ran: talking idly
blink: a while, moment
blue-boram: English slang for syphilis
boddle: old copper coin (worth two Scottish pennies)
bogle: hobgoblin
bonie (bony): bonny, beautiful
bonnock: thick cake of bread or oatmeal
boord: board
boord-en': head of the table
boortries: shrub-elder
bore: small hole
botch: angry tumour
bousing: drinking
brae: slope of a hill, river bank
braid: broad
brash: sudden, brief illness
brats: small pieces, rags, children
brattle: short race, hurry
braw: handsome, finely dressed
breeks: breeches
brunstane: brimstone
buckler: helmet strap
bumman: humming
burnewin: blacksmith
buskit: well dressed
butt an' ben: kitchen and parlour
byke: beehive

cadie: messenger
callor: fresh, cool
cantharidian: of cantharides, Spanish fly (aphrodisiac)

cantie: cheerful, lively
cantraip: spell, charm
cape-stane: copestone, keystone
carlin: stout old woman
cauld: cold
caup: wooden cup
cesses: taxes
chantan: chanting
chapman billies: pedlar fellows
chow: to chew
chuffie: fat-faced
claes (claise): clothes
claithing: clothing
clatter: an idle story
claymore: sword
cleekit: linked together
clinkumbell: church bell-ringer
cog: wooden dish
collieshangie: quarrelling
cood: cud
coof: blockhead, ninny
cootie: wooden dish
cotter: inhabitant of a cottage
coulter: iron blade at front of a ploughshare
countra: country
cour: fold, duck down
cranreuch: hoar-frost
craps: crop
creeshie: greasy
croose: proud, cocksure
crowdie: oatmeal with water, or milk
crowdie-time: breakfast-time, mealtime
crowlan: crawling
crummock: crooked-horned cow
crump: hard, brittle (of bread)
curchie: curtsy
cushat: dove or wood pigeon

daffin: merriment
dail: plank
daimen-icker: occasional ear of corn
daur: to dare
daut: to fondle, caress
dawd: large portion
dawtet: fondled
deave: to deafen
deil: devil
dight: to wipe
ding: to excel, surpass
dinna: do not
ditty: reproof
dool: sorrow
dorty: saucy
doup-skelper: bottom-slapper
douse: sober, wise, prudent
dow: can
dowff: lacking in spirit
dowie: sad, lonesome
doylt: stupid, crazed
droddum: breech, backside
droukit: soaked, drenched
drumlie: muddy
dub: pool, puddle
duds: rags
dung: worsted, subdued
dunts: blows
durk: dagger
dyvors: bankrupts

e'e: eye
een: eyes, evening
eldritch: frightful
Embro: Edinburgh
ettle: to try, intent

fa': fall
faem: foam
fairing: desserts, present from a fair
farl: cake of bread or oats
fash: trouble, care
fatt'rels: ribbon ends
fausont: decent
fechtin: fighting
feck: many, plenty, the greater bulk
fell: keen, biting
ferlie: wonder, to marvel
fient: fiend
flaffan: flapping
flainen: flannel
foggage: coarse grass grown for winter feed
fou: full, drunk
frae: from
fu': full
furm: form, wooden bench
furr: furrow
fyke: to fret, in a fuss

gaed: went
gane: gone
gar: to make, to compel
gash: wise
gat: got, received
gate: way, manner
gaunt: to yawn
gawsie: jolly, large
gaylies: adequately, pretty well
gear: goods, wealth
get: a child, issue
gie: to give
gill: Scots measure
gin: if, by, against
gizz: face
glaikit: foolish

glib-gabbet: smooth-talking
glintan: shining briefly
glunch: to frown
gowan: daisy, dandelion
gowd: gold
grain: to groan
graith: harness, equipment
greetan: weeping
greives: farm overseer
groat: small coin
grozet: gooseberry
grutten: wept
gude-willie-waught: a drink with great good will
guid: good
guidman: master of the house
guidwife: mistress of the house

ha': hall
haffet: side of the head, temple
hafflins: halfway
hald: hold, resting place
hallions: rascals, rogues
hame: home
hap-step-an'-loup: hop, skip and leap
harn: coarse linen
haughs: low-lying meadow
hawkie: cow
hearse: hoarse
herriet: robbed
het: hot
heugh: hollow
hirplan: creeping, limping
histie: dry, barren
hizzy: hussy
hoast: cough
hoddan: hobbling
hodden: coarse grey woollen cloth
houghmagandie: fornication

houlet: owl
howcket: digged
howe: hollow, dale
hurdies: hips, buttocks

ilka: each, every

jad: jade, worthless nag
jaup: to splash
jink: to dodge
jinkan: dodging
jo: sweetheart

kae: jackdaw
kebbuck: cheese
keek: to peep
keekit: peeped
ken: to know
kent: knew
ket: fleece
kintra (kintry): country
kintra cooser: travelling stallion
kirk: church
kirn: churn
kittle: to tickle
knowe: hillock
kyte: belly

laith: loath
lanely: lonely
lave: the rest, the others
lav'rock: lark
lear: learning
leeze me: a phrase of congratulation or endearment
leuk: to look
libbet: castrated
linkan: tripping
linket: tripped

loof: palm of the hand
lough: lake
lour: look threateningly, impending
lowan: flaming
lowe: flame
lowp: to leap
lug: ear
luggies: wooden dish with handles
lyart: grey

mailen: farm
maist: most
manteele: mantle
mashlum: mixed corn
maukin: hare
maun: must
mell: to meddle
melvie: to soil with meal
mense: manners, decorum
mim: prim
moil: labour
mony (monie): many
mou: mouth
muckle: great, big
mutchkin: English pint

na: not
nane: none
nappy: ale
neist: next
neuk (newk): nook, corner
nieve: fist
nit: nut
nowt: cattle

ony (onie): any
owrehip: overarm hammer strike

painch: stomach
pattle: plough spade
penny-wheep: small beer
phiz: face
pirratch: porridge
plack: old Scottish coin (worth one third of a Scottish penny)
plackless: penniless
pleugh-pettle: plough-staff
pliskie: trick
poin'd: to seize
poortith: poverty
pou'd: pulled
pow: head

queir: choir

raep: rope
raible: to talk nonsense
rass-buss: bush of rushes
rattlan: rattling
raucle: rash, fearless
rax: to stretch
ream: to froth
reaming: brimful, frothing
reck: to heed
rede: to advise, counsel
red-wud: stark mad
reek: to smoke, smoke
reekan: smoking
reekit: smoked
reestet: scorched
remead: remedy
rigwoodie: coarse, tough
rin: to run
rive: to burst
roupet: hoarse, with a cold
rowe: to roll, to wrap
rowth: abundance

rozet: rosin
rung: cudgel
runkl'd: wrinkled

sae: so
sair: sore
sairly: sorely
sark: shirt
saunt: saint
saut: salt
scaud: to scald
scaur: to scare
sconner: to loathe, loathing
scrievin: gliding gleefully
shoon: shoes
sic: such
simmer: summer
skellum: worthless fellow
skelp: slap, to run
skelpan: walking quickly, often barefoot
skelpit: hurried forward
skinking: watery, thin soup
skirl: to shriek
sklentan: slanted
slae: sloe
slap: gate
sma': small
smeddum: medicinal powder
smoutie: smutty, sooty
snawy: snowy
sned: to cut off
snell: bitter
snick-drawing: trick-conniving
snool: to cringe, sneak, submit
sonsie: jolly, ample
souple: supple, flexible
spail: splinters
spairge: to soil, bespatter

spean: to wean
speel: to climb
spence: parlour
spier: to ask, inquire
splore: a frolic, a riot
squttle: to squat
staw: stole
steek: to shut
stell: a still
sten: to leap, to rear as a horse
stents: tributes
stoor: hollow sounding
stoure: dust in motion, excitement, commotion
stowp: measuring jug for serving liquids
strunt: to swagger
sugh: light breeze, heavy sigh
swaird: sward, smooth grass
swat: sweated
swatch: sample
swats: good ale
swith: swift
syne: since, then

tapsalteerie: topsy-turvy
tauk: talk
tauted: matted together
tent: field pulpit, to take care
tentless: careless
teugh: tough
thairm: intestines
thegither: together
thiggin: begging
thole: to suffer
thowes: thaws
thrang: throng, busy
thrave: twenty-four sheaves of corn
thrissle: thistle
thy-lane: on your own

tine: to lose
tint: lost
tirl: to uncover, to strip
tirlan: uncovering
tittlan: whispering
toolzie: fight, squabble
toom: empty
tow: rope
towmont: year (a twelvemonth)
towzie: shaggy, unkempt
toy: old-fashioned woman's headdress
trow: to believe
twa: two
twalt: the twelfth
twathree: two or three, a few
twin: to part, give up
tyke: dog

unco: very, uncouth, strange
usquabae: water of life, whisky

vauntie: vain, proud

wad: would, to wager
wae: woe, sad
waesucks: alas
wale: choice, the best
walie: large, jolly
wame: the belly
wanchancie: unlucky
war'd: to lay out
warl (warld): world
warly: worldly
wat: know, wet
water-fit: river mouth
wauken: to wake
waur: worse, to worst
wean (weanies): child

weel: well
westlin: westerly
whang: leather string, piece of cheese or bread, to flog
whittle: knife
whun-stane: whinstone, any hard, compact rock, such as basalt
whyles: sometimes
wight: strong, clever
wimplin: meandering
winnock: window
winnock-bunker: window-seat
wonner: wonder
worm: spiral tube on a still
wud: mad
wylecoat: flannel vest
wyling: beguiling, enticing
wyte: blame

yell: dry
yestreen: yesterday evening
yett: gate
yeukin: itching
yill: ale

Index of First Lines